Searching for Mr. Chin

SEARCHING FOR MR. CHIN

Constructions of Nation and the Chinese in West Indian Literature

ANNE-MARIE LEE-LOY

Temple University Press
PHILADELPHIA

Temple University Press
Philadelphia, Pennsylvania 19122
www.temple.edu/tempress

Pubilshed 2010
Printed in the United States of America

♾ The paper used in this publication meets the requirements of the American National Standard for Information Sciences—Permanence of Paper for Printed Library Materials, ANSI Z39.48-1992

LIBRARY OF CONGRESS CATALOGING-IN-PUBLICATION DATA

Lee-Loy, Anne-Marie.
Searching for Mr. Chin : constructions of nation and the Chinese in West Indian literature / Anne-Marie Lee-Loy.
p. cm.
Includes bibliographical references and index.
ISBN 978-1-4399-0130-4 (cloth : alk. paper)
ISBN 978-1-4399-0132-8 (electronic)
1. West Indian fiction (English)—20th century—History and criticism. 2. Chinese in literature. 3. West Indian fiction (English)—Chinese influences. 4. National characteristics in literature. I. Title.
PR9214.L44 2010
813'.009'9729—dc22

2009052964

110519P

THE AMERICAN LITERATURES INITIATIVE

A book in the American Literatures Initiative (ALI), a collaborative publishing project of NYU Press, Fordham University Press, Rutgers University Press, Temple University Press, and the University of Virginia Press. The Initiative is supported by The Andrew W. Mellon Foundation. For more information, please visit www.americanliteratures.org.

Contents

CONTENTS

For my parents

Acknowledgments

I have had the good fortune to be surrounded by an incredibly supportive community of colleagues, friends, and family throughout my work on this project. I must first acknowledge David Dabydeen who originally challenged me to consider this topic and has consistently supported me at various stages of this work. Clem Seecharan and John Gilmore were also influential early on, challenging me to push the boundaries of my thinking by asking hard questions and being willing to engage in thoughtful discussion. Walton Look Lai and Keith Lowe were in many ways early mentors, and I am grateful for the time, advice, and expertise that they have generously shared and for their enthusiasm for this work. I also express my gratitude to Victor Chang, Willi Chen, Easton Lee, and Janice Lowe Shinebourne, who, with a mixture of insightfulness and humor, were willing to share with me their thoughts (and on occasion, a good meal!) on the myriad ways of "being Chinese" in the West Indies. The careful, detailed, and thought-provoking comments of the two anonymous readers of this manuscript must also be acknowledged. Their attentive readings did much to help me clarify my thinking and shape the final organization of this research.

I am deeply grateful for the professional guidance, support, and patience of the staff at Temple University Press and the American Literatures Initiative, especially my editorial team Janet Francendese, Emily Taber, and Tim Roberts. The diligence and detailed professionalism of Teresa Jesionowski and the willingness of Lisa Kozak and Alexia Citak to proofread and edit this manuscript at various stages are much appreciated. I also thank Martin Mordecai and Joan Camps-Campins for graciously granting permission to reproduce their work, Ilka Hilton-Clarke of the Art Society of Trinidad and Tobago for all her advice and ideas, and the staff at the Bodleian and British Newspaper Libraries and the Public Record Office for their professionalism and patience. I must recognize Reverend and Mrs. Gordon Evans, Reverend Maitland Evans and family, Kellie-Ann Evans-Hall, Simone Schloss, and Jeneen Raymond as well. They showed great kindness and hospitality on my trip to Jamaica and helped to make this research experience enjoyable as well as thorough.

I consider myself lucky to work in an institution that prizes collegiality as well as teaching and research excellence. I appreciate the support that my department has given throughout this project and the interest that my colleagues have shown in the progress of this research. I must, however, single out the always witty Randy Boyagoda who initially searched for (and found) Mr. Chin. I also acknowledge a circle of friends whose interest in this project has never (outwardly!) waned. They include David Chariandy, Marlene Pinto, Monique Rajaram, and Sharon Stewart Guthrie. I so appreciate the safe spaces you created in which I could work out many of my ideas.

I owe an immeasurable debt to my family. Of my supportive extended family, I particularly thank my uncle, Vincent Lee, for courageously opening up new worlds to me, and I acknowledge the warm hospitality of the Lees in South Dakota. My sister, Ingrid, has been an amazing networking resource, while my brother, Irwin, helped keep me grounded with his weird and wonderful sense of humor. Siân and Sam have been incredibly patient with me throughout this project. I am even more grateful for the laughter they bring to my day and am ever inspired by the curiosity and joy with which they greet the world. I thank my husband, David, for the many ways he showed his support for this project, especially for taking on all those mundane and thankless tasks that kept our household running when I was preoccupied or distracted. And finally, I thank my parents, Samuel and Genevieve Lee-Loy. Words are sorely inadequate to express my gratitude for the innumerable sacrifices they have made to help their children achieve their dreams and the unconditional support and love with which they have always surrounded us.

Searching for Mr. Chin

Introduction

Chinyman
He moves haphazardly, blown along the pavement
In uneven gusts, like rice paper.
The oldest man in the world.
Not for him, beneath the mask of grey
Enamelled hair, dried dreams of palaces
Floating on their pools of silken poetry
Or orchideous concubines in rites of silk.
More likely a drab exchange of servitude,
Eastern soil for saltfish,
And the crudely offered tithes paid daily
On the mackerel counters by us lazy blacks
Who'd rather spend than sell;
The necessary sacrifice of language
And the timeless shame of burial
In this uncultured soil.
Yet in this intricate embroidery of that face
Are all the possibilities of legend:
Kublai Khan in beggar's garb.

Loub-limbed and less immediately ancient
I defer the pavement to this parchment schooner
With no port, this ivory chorale of semitones.

—MARTIN MORDECAI

If Martin Mordecai's poem "Chinyman" seems familiar on first reading, it is hardly surprising. The poem is built, after all, around a sense of jarring dislocation concerning the presence of a Chinese man in the West Indies, and the Chinese are not often the first ethnic community that comes to mind when one thinks of West Indian spaces.[1] Indeed, the poem's imagery suggests that the Chinese man is not only displaced but that his presence in the West Indies is extremely tenuous: he moves "haphazardly," is deemed "port-less," and is so rootless that he is likely to be blown away as easily as parchment paper. He is, as the poem suggests, the false note in his environment. And yet, the picture of Chinese alienation that Mordecai so effectively constructs is subtly undermined in the poem's closing lines when the narrator defers his own place on the pavement to make room for the Chinese man. In this moment of accommodation, the ideas of estrangement and dislocation in which "Chineseness" has been constructed throughout the poem are subverted: apparently, there *is* room for the Chinese man in the West Indies. Thus, Chineseness as embodied by the "Chinyman" becomes a site of ambiguity, caught in the tension of belonging and nonbelonging; and it is this ambiguity pertaining to the literary representations of the Chinese in Jamaica, Trinidad, and Guyana that is the focus of this book.

To consider the question of belonging and nonbelonging in relation to Chinese West Indians is not, of course, abstract. Instead, belonging is located in the greater concept of nation. This book examines fiction produced in the West Indies from the earliest part of the twentieth century until contemporary times as a means of exploring and understanding the strategies and agendas behind the ways in which the Chinese are imagined within the greater construction of West Indian nationhood. At its simplest, the question at the heart of this study is: What do twentieth-century fictional images of the Chinese reveal about the construction and articulation of nationhood in the former West Indian colonies?

Before addressing this question, we must start with another: Why the nation? After all, has not the nation become irrelevant in this globalized era? Have we not been challenged to "think ourselves beyond the nation"?[2] Certainly, as many scholars have pointed out, national borders seem to be blurring as individuals, capital, ideas, and loyalties criss-cross the globe. Nevertheless, despite such mobility and seeming permeability of national borders, these borders have not disappeared. Indeed, as I write this chapter, new rules have just been instituted at the world's longest unguarded border, that between Canada and the United States, which, for the first time, require all Canadians to show their passports before entering the United States.[3] National borders are apparently not only still in existence but are becoming more clearly defined.

The rupture in the academic debate over the existence of the nation and its future lies in a tension between the political and the cultural. Whether or not one believes that the nation is on the wane often relates to whether or not one is speaking about a political entity or a more cultural concept. The nation-state, that political body that controls borders, may be facing new challenges to its power, but the nation as a cultural identity continues to have a powerful hold on our imaginations. One need only think of the Olympic Games to see this tension clearly: many of the competitors train and live in different nations from the one under whose flag they proudly compete.

My examination of West Indian nationhood investigates a cultural phenomenon and a social practice. It seeks to map and understand a cultural process of identity formation: "Chineseness" in the West Indies. Thus, the subject matter under investigation is essentially cultural production. Additionally, many of the texts to be explored were written in the early- and mid-twentieth century when the colonies were moving steadily toward independence. It was a period in which an awareness of nationhood was a central component of the sociopolitical environment. Such texts are often particularly interested in revealing or participating in the process of nation-building. Finally, whether or not the nation-state exists today in the form in which it was understood to exist in the early twentieth century, the relationships between individuals within (former) nation-states have long-term implications. In the same way that the implications of colonialism are still being felt long after the colonies ceased to exist as political units, the relationships between Chinese and other West Indians that were founded when the concept of the nation was more secure do not just disappear even if the idea of nation itself has changed. Thus, nation remains an appropriate—perhaps even the best—context against which this exploration into images of Chineseness in the West Indies takes place.

The moment of encounter between the Chinyman and the speaker in Mordecai's poem—an encounter that is not only literal but also represents a coming together of ideas and images—that ambiguous moment when various narratives of Chineseness collide to produce "all the possibilities of legend" is suggestive of my overall approach to this study. I want to foreground an understanding of nation space as a creative "zone of instability" within which writers work with "multiple, heterogeneous, and in many cases contradictory discourses and practices" in shaping their production of the nation's cultural identity.[4] As will be discussed in more detail in the subsequent chapter, these discourses and practices are directly related to the conditions of modernity in which West Indian nations came into being. In particular, because they are formerly colonized countries intensely aware of their global connections, some of the foundational concepts of modern national identities, such as a belief in mythic links between landscape, history, and culture as the basis of an organically emerging cultural identity, are destabilized. This destabilization renders the nation an intrinsically unfinished "problematic" and those narratives that establish who belongs in the nation to be equally unfinished.[5] What I am interested in, however, is not the inherent ambiguity of nation caught in the act of self-mythologization; that is, I am not interested in exposing the falseness of a homogenous nation-self as the ultimate product of national narrative. Instead, I want to connect the ambiguity of the concept of nation directly to the multiplicity of narratives that are employed in the articulation of national identity as a state of belonging. In emphasizing this multiplicity, I want to consider the ambiguous images of Chinese belonging that appear in West Indian literature as a product of the varied ways in which belonging and nonbelonging for West Indian nations in general are imagined. There is more than one way to imagine the boundaries of national belonging, and the fictional images of the Chinese capture this inherent instability.

Historical Context of Ambiguous Belonging

NINETEENTH-CENTURY CHINESE MIGRATION TO THE WEST INDIES

The ambiguous images of Chineseness in relation to nationhood that appear in West Indian literature arise not only from the peculiar pressures of modern nationhood. The particular migration history of the Chinese has also contributed to the instability surrounding the roles in which they are cast in national narratives. Chinese migration to the West Indies began in the nineteenth century as an indentured labor phenomenon and was therefore intrinsically intertwined with colonial ambitions to maintain the plantation economies that were the foundation of their power and privilege. These economies had, however, been significantly disrupted when the slaves were emancipated in 1833 and their mandatory apprenticeships concluded five years later. A further shake-up for the sugar industry, the backbone of the West Indian economy, had occurred in 1846 when the Sugar Duties Act was passed, removing measures that had protected West Indian–produced sugar from competition with other sugar sources, including European beet sugar and sugar produced by slaves elsewhere, most notably in Cuba. These two blows, often coupled with soil depletion on plantations, caused the sugar industry to fall into such severe decline that by 1850, it could be claimed that sugar estates in the West Indies had devalued an incredible 90 percent in a ten-year period, and that three-fourths of West Indian planters were on the verge of absolute financial ruin.[6]

Despite the impact of these significant changes in the world sugar market and, in some cases, the damage to West Indian soil caused by the overproduction of sugar, the dire financial state in which the colonies found themselves by the mid-nineteenth century was commonly blamed on a perceived lack of controlled labor on the sugar estates since slave emancipation. Planters sought a new source of labor that, while allowing the laborer to be nominally free, would provide them with controls over the workforce similar to those they had wielded during slavery. Indentured labor, which provided measures to control mobility and directly addressed absenteeism in its contracts, soon appeared to be the solution to this problem, or as one writer put it more poetically:

> Immigration to this province may be likened to supplying with water a reservoir employed to afford power to extensive mechanical appliances; when the supply is abundant, the machinery will work up to its full power; but, when it proves to be deficient, when the source is obstructed by any circumstances, the water in the reservoir will sink below its working level and the machinery will stop.[7]

China was just one of a number of locations that the colonial government considered as a potential source for indentured labor. Eventually, India would become the primary—and perhaps most well-known—source of such labor; nevertheless, Chinese indentured labor precedes that from India when, in 1806, 192 Chinese arrived in Trinidad to work on the sugar estates. This first batch of Chinese indentured laborers would not, however, form the real basis upon which the Chinese populations of the West Indies would be founded. Indeed, most of these migrants left upon the completion of their contracts. It has been estimated that as early as 1809 only thirty Chinese were left on the island, with this number dwindling to about a dozen by 1825.[8] Interest in the Chinese as potential indentured laborers for the West Indies would not be revived until the 1840s, although actual indentured labor migration did not recommence until 1853.

The bulk of Chinese indentured labor migration to the West Indies occurred between 1853 and 1866. This migration did not, however, continue in a steady stream over this period. For example, the three-year period between 1855 and 1858 saw no Chinese migrants enter the colonies. Nevertheless, by the end of the nineteenth century, some 18,000 Chinese would arrive in the West Indies, with the vast majority of those migrants (around

75 percent) headed for Guyana. As was the case with most migration out of China in the nineteenth century, the immigrants were drawn from southern China and were seeking to escape desperate conditions caused by a combination of environmental catastrophes and political unrest. Canton (Guangzhou) provided many of the immigrants, although Swatow (Shantou) and Amoy (Xiamen) were eventually considered more valuable centers in terms of recruiting the type of people who were thought to be good laborers as opposed to what one observer described as "the worthless population of the towns."[9] The migrants were a diverse group that included individuals from a variety of ethnic groups and social and economic classes. Members of the Hakka, Punti, and Hok Lo ethnic groups have been specifically identified as participating in the migration, and it was suggested that there were representatives from 150 occupations, including doctors and schoolmasters, among the migrants in the colony.[10] There were also a considerable number of Christian converts among the migrants as a result of the colonial government's willingness to rely on Christian missionaries to assist them in their recruitment endeavors, particularly in the recruiting of family units.[11]

The use of Christian missionaries in recruitment was just one of many measures that the colonial government used in its bid to avoid accusations that indenture was simply slavery under a new name. The government was particularly sensitive to such accusations because it was competing directly with other European powers, particularly Spain, to recruit laborers from China. In general, the recruitment of Chinese laborers was done by professional recruiters, known as "crimps," who were paid per individual recruit, while the recruits themselves received a cash advance. Arnold J. Meagher argues that although the use of crimps to recruit Chinese labor had emerged in the first half of the nineteenth century, it was not until the late 1850s when both the demand for Chinese labor and the fees paid to crimps had increased dramatically that the system became notorious for its association with abuse and coercion, including kidnapping. Indeed, so bad was the perception of crimp-controlled migration that it was said to be known among the Chinese as "the sale of Little Pigs," a particularly vivid means of capturing the lack of choice that many of the "migrants" had with regard to their migration and the inhumane treatment that they often faced. This "recruitment," along with the treatment that the migrants received, deteriorated so much that in 1874, a Chinese commission was sent to Cuba to investigate the conditions of the Chinese there. Their findings would ultimately end Chinese indentured labor on that island.[12]

In contrast, Chinese indentured immigration to the British West Indies had been permitted only under the condition that the colonial government would retain control over the process (as opposed to allowing it to be run by individual prospectors), and by 1859, the period in which the most organized and heaviest indentured migration from China began, a different recruitment system from that being used by Spain had been established. This system relied on British immigration officials who, with the assistance of Chinese officials, worked out of emigration houses where migrants were interviewed before leaving the country as a means of ensuring that they were migrating of their own free will.[13]

Through various ordinances, the colonial government's involvement in Chinese indentured labor migration extended far beyond recruitment. For example, ordinances were passed that determined the size of the ships that could carry migrants to the colonies while others specified the rights and responsibilities of both laborer and estate management upon the migrants' arrival in the colonies. Indeed, on a superficial level, the government involvement seemed to ensure that the migrants were well-treated,

> . . . provided with free house-room, regular work and wages when they are in health, and in sickness have the advantages of a hospital, the attendance of a medical man and medicines free of expense, who have moreover a magistrate always at hand to hear their complaints and a department of officers with especial duty of securing their good treatment.[14]

Nevertheless, the indenture system was not immune from accusations that it perpetrated a new slavery. Despite the Colonial Office's precautions, for example, the recruitment process was still suspect. Mr. Sampson, the emigration agent in Canton during the 1860s, noted that despite the care he took in processing migrants, he knew of at least one instance of "a tolerably clear case of kidnapping" that had almost escaped his notice, suggesting that it was certainly possible for other unwilling migrants to have passed through the system.[15] Even more troubling was the practice of providing additional advance money for women migrants, a measure introduced because it was believed that it was only with such an incentive that Chinese females could be induced or permitted to participate in the migration. Although the initial proposal had been greeted negatively with the fear that such a practice would provide an "opening for the greatest abuses, and in fact to set on foot a trade little different from the Slave Trade," the advancement of such money was eventually allowed.[16] Those fears seemed to have been more than justified as a significant proportion of Chinese women brought to the colonies were described variously as "refuse" and

> . . . mere outcasts, filled into the ships by Chinese agency from the dregs of Chinese life, and in such respect of age and personal defects and infirmities, that to enumerate them in the proportion of women required for the help and solace of men seems like little better than mockery.[17]

The ship's surgeon on the *Whirlwind* was even more specific when he described the female migrants on his ship as consisting of "two notorious prostitutes, four idiots, one helpless cripple—one hunchback—one deaf and dumb, and several much disfigured by scars," and the 1862 Report of the Agent General of Immigrants in Trinidad complained that "for the most part [the Chinese migrants had] repudiated the wives whom they picked up at Hong Kong . . . with a view of sharing in or appropriating their advance money."[18]

Two of the most well known nineteenth-century criticisms

of indentured labor in the West Indies were an 1871 pamphlet entitled *The New Slavery: An Account of the Indian and Chinese Immigrants in British Guiana* and a letter by G. William Des Voeux, a former magistrate in British Guiana, to the then colonial secretary, Lord Granville. In his somewhat spontaneous letter, Des Voeux claimed that the indentured laborers were so badly treated in British Guiana that the colony faced imminent revolution. In response, the Colonial Office established a royal commission charged with investigating two main points: first, whether the indentured laborers had been recruited under false promises of the wages they could make and the conditions under which they would labor and, second, whether or not the legal system in the colony was so biased that the laborers were unable to get justice and the legal provisions designed to protect them were, as such, ineffectual.

Despite the commissioners' somewhat patronizing attitude toward the indentured laborers and their biased assumption that all "Asiatics" were inherently given to untruth and exaggeration, their report provides considerable insight into the distressful conditions faced by the immigrants, ranging from a failure to make promised wages, to poor housing and medical care, to the extremely harsh penal provisions for breaches of contract. Also striking is the revelation of the casual violence that marked their everyday lives. For example, the commissioners were particularly disturbed to hear of the murder of one Low-A-Si, an indentured laborer on Plantation Annandale, who after refusing to work, either due to bad health or fatigue, was beaten to death by the head overseer and the driver. Indeed, following the commission's investigation, one observer was forced to conclude:

> Politically, we have ascertained, the Coolie is nil; he has no voice, nor the shadow of a voice, in the government of British Guiana. Socially he is not only a laborer, he is a bondsman—using the word in no invidious sense—he is not free to come and go, to work and rest, as he pleases.[19]

One of the complaints addressed by the commissioners was the lack of provision for back passage (that is, return passage) for the Chinese migrants in their contracts. Some of the Chinese laborers had claimed that, like the migrants from India, back passage had been promised to them by recruiters in China. Although the commissioners ultimately decided that such promises had never been made, the issue of back passages would continue to be a sore point that would eventually play a key role in ending Chinese indentured labor to the West Indies. In 1866, the Kung Convention signed in China, but never ratified in Britain, specifically provided back passage provisions for the Chinese laborers. West Indian planters were not, however, prepared to cover the additional cost that this would incur, especially in light of the fact that India was proving more than sufficient as a source of migrant labor. After the Chinese government refused to back down on the provision, interest in the Chinese as indentured laborers seems to have simply faded. Indeed, after 1866, only three vessels of Chinese indentured laborers would arrive in the West Indies: two to Guyana and one to Jamaica.

COLONIAL DISCOURSE AND NINETEENTH-CENTURY REPRESENTATIONS OF CHINESENESS

The manner in which the colonial powers introduced the Chinese into the West Indies and the socioeconomic roles that they afforded to the migrants would directly affect how the Chinese were imagined and represented in colonial discourse in terms of where they belonged in the West Indies' social, economic, and political landscapes. Indeed, these images reveal a long-term ambivalence in representing the Chinese as belonging in the region. Much of this ambivalence arises from what Homi K. Bhabha memorably described as the "forked tongue" of colonial discourse. In that image, Bhabha vividly captured the tension engendered by the disconnect between British colonialism's avowed moral project—its "civilizing mission"—and its desire to retain the unequal power hierarchies of colonial societies. Bhabha concluded that, produced at "the intersection between European learning and colonial power," the colonized

Other becomes a subject of "double articulation"—that is, a "forked tongue"—represented as both having and not having the potential to actually become "civilized."[20]

Colonial images of the Chinese in the West Indies display a similar doubling. For example, one of the most overused images in colonial documents considering Chinese indentured migration to the West Indies was that of the Chinese as an inherently gentle and submissive people: as a "cheerful, peaceable and well-disposed" people who demonstrate "docility and obedience," as well as "regular order, obedience and industry, together with a perfect degree of reconciliation, confidence and happiness"; and, importantly, as being "too sensible to be led away into riots."[21] This image is, however, destabilized by the concurrent tales of Chinese violence, including the violence directed at those involved in the recruitment of Chinese laborers and the numerous mutinies on the ships carrying the laborers to the Americas.[22] Similarly, the popular colonial depiction of the Chinese as a particularly industrious people who would save the plantations through their "indefatigable industry" and "indomitable industry and perseverance" is subverted by complaints that the Chinese laborers were too "independent"—that is, less submissive and controllable—in terms of their attitude toward estate management[23]. For example, one of the observers of the royal commission recounts how, during a tour of a sugar plantation, he and the manager came across an apparently healthy Chinese male who was not working but merely amusing himself with a group of Chinese ladies. When the manager makes a subtle hint that the Chinese man should be working, the laborer responds coolly, "No. No think work."[24] The moment is significant for the negative tone in which it is related. It reveals that by removing himself from the role accorded to him in colonial discourses, namely as an industrious laborer, this unnamed Chinese man also removes himself from being represented as having a valid place in the West Indies. There were also complaints that the Chinese were particularly prone to absconding from the estates. Indeed, one of the concerns raised regarding the 1865 establishment of Hopetown, a free Chinese village in Guyana, was that it would prove a haven and a goal for runaway laborers. The apparently high rate of suicide for the Chinese during this period can also be read as an act of resistance against the harsh and denigrating labor situation in which they found themselves.

The instability in the representation of the Chinese is particularly apparent in the uneven way in which ideas of Chinese assimilation to British norms and values were articulated in colonial discourse. Great attention was paid, for example, to evidence of Chinese conversion to Christianity. This is perhaps not surprising since one of the colonial justifications for Chinese indentured labor was the claim that exposure to Christianity would inevitably, in some never clearly explained fashion, bring about the conversion of the migrants. It was confidently stated, for example, that once in the West Indies, the Chinese would "very soon from Conviction embrace a persuasion established in the Divine Principles of General and Universal Benevolence and Charity in preference to a Continuance in their own Incongruous and [illegible word] Doctrines"; "unlearn something of the practices of their own country, and be brought into contact with the influences of Christianity and of a civilization comparatively European"; and "under the influence of a civilized condition of a society, forego their home and forget their gods."[25] More specifically:

> The defenders of the Asiatic immigration to the West Indies have always been careful to point out, besides the material advantages offered to the immigrant, the prospect of moral improvement which it opened to the races. It has been held upon as a means of carrying Western civilization and even Western faith to the nations of India and China.[26]

The conversion of the "Heathen Chinee" was therefore understood to confirm the superiority of European civilization and culture, which, in turn, also confirmed the social and cultural hierarchy of the colonies.[27] Thus, as early as 1853 an explicit link between positive representations of the Chinese in the West Indies and their involvement with Christianity was being made. In Guyana, Governor Henry Barkly enthused that the first Chinese immigrants were "participating in the services at a missionary chapel," a fact that led directly to his conclusion that "the Chinese [possess] the energy and the intelligence attributed to them."[28] More typically, favorable representations of the Chinese were grounded in a comparison with the migrants from India who were proving less amenable to conversion. It was even explicitly suggested that China was a better source of emigrants than India because the Chinese seemed more willing to accept Christian instruction, while one missionary based his description of the Chinese as "pious" and "*gentil*" on the amount of the money they were willing to offer the church.[29] A newspaper article reporting on an execution of two migrants, one Indian and the other one Chinese, provided colonialists with a more dramatic contrast between supposed Indian and Chinese attitudes toward Christianity. On their last night alive, the Indian migrant refused to listen to any clergyman and spent his final hours dancing in his cell; in contrast, the Chinese prisoner spent the night attentively listening to the prayers of the Roman Catholic priest who would eventually accompany him on the scaffold.[30] That such a story would even make the news suggests how important the image of Chinese conversion was to colonial discourses that sought to justify and maintain the power structures within their societies.

The possibility of assimilation and, thereby, of belonging in the West Indies that is suggested in the representation of the Chinese converts also extended outside of religious matters. Other depictions of the Chinese during this period take particular care to present the Chinese as absorbing other aspects of European cultural norms and values. In this regard, a surprising amount of attention is given in colonial texts to reporting that the Chinese community was willing to dress in accordance with European standards of fashion. For example, during his tour of Trinidad, Charles Kingsley records his encounter with a group of Chinese women who were not only attending a church service but were attired in expensive European-styled finery, and in Guyana, Barkly was pleased to report that the Chinese were apparently purchasing articles of European clothing. Another example of the importance given to representing the Chinese as assimilating to European values can be found in the memoirs of Henry Kirke, a former sheriff of Demerara. Kirke recounts a story of attending a dinner hosted by a Chinese man where he was impressed to note that he was served Hennessy XXX brandy. More important in this regard, Kirke also details his host's reaction to the suggestion that Chinese eat dogs. The man became quite agitated, insisting that only "bad" Chinese do so. This division between "good" and "bad" Chinese on the grounds of whether or not they behaved in accordance with European standards of behavior suggests that the host understood well the terms under which the Chinese could be represented as "good" within nineteenth-century West Indian colonial discourse. Simply put, the "good Chinese" were the assimilated Chinese; and only the "good Chinese" could belong in the West Indies.

Despite such images, colonial discourse never pictured the Chinese as fully assimilated, subverting its own discursive constructs with contemporaneous images of Chinese unassimilability. This strategy of portraying the Chinese as "almost the same, *but not quite*" reaffirmed the continued lower status of the Chinese to the European elements of West Indian society; the Chinese are never their peers.[31] These images also affected perceptions of Chinese belonging, for, by representing them as unassimilable and exotic, such images reified cultural difference as the key factor in marking out the Chinese as outsiders in West Indian space. Thus, nineteenth-century newspaper articles spent considerable time reporting on Chinese dietary choices, suggesting that they ate frogs, cats, rats, and, of course, dogs, while other writers of the period insisted that the Chinese were actually not giving up traditional styles of clothing or traditional ways of eating with chopsticks.[32] Such images essentially depict the Chinese as an alien presence in West Indian societies to the extent that Chinese alienation became a literary trope.

Indeed, so recognizable was this image, that Kingsley easily used it in his own work. Specifically, Kingsley recounts attending the races in Trinidad where he was disturbed by the amount of rum and general frivolity that he observed. In his account, Kingsley is careful to note the presence of a Chinese man who, like Kingsley, remains at a physical distance from the boisterous crowd. Although the two men do not apparently engage in conversation, Kingsley insists that the Chinese man is "absorbed in the very same reflection" that he is.[33] In doing so, the Chinese man becomes the embodiment of Kingsley's own feelings of alienation and a figure whose presence intensifies the sense of estrangement with which Kingsley paints the scene.

Ultimately, in colonial discourse, ambivalence regarding Chinese belonging was connected to whether or not the migrants were perceived as supporting the colonial order. Indeed, in this regard, the most important colonial image of the Chinese was as an in-between, "middleman" community within the hierarchical social order of the colonies, who, thus positioned, would maintain the plantations through their labor and their ability to neutralize political discontent. This role is made obvious from the earliest colonial discussions of possible Chinese migration to the West Indies.

> The events which have recently happened at St. Domingo [Haiti] necessarily awakes all those apprehensions which the establishment of a Negro government in that island gave rise to some years ago and render it indispensable that every practicable measure of precaution should be adopted to guard the British possessions in the West Indies as well against any future indisposition of power so constituted as against the danger of a spirit of insurrection being excited amongst the Negroes in our colonies.
>
> It is conceived that no measure would so effectually tend to provide a security against this danger, as that of introducing a free race of cultivators into our islands, who, from habits and feelings would be kept distinct from the

> Negroes, and who from interest would be inseparably attached to European proprietors.
>
> The Chinese people are represented to unite the qualities which constitute this double recommendation.[34]

Thus, Chinese indentured labor was described as "one of the best possible schemes" specifically because the presence of the Chinese in the colony was depicted as providing "a barrier between us and the negroes" and as "*form[ing] a middle class* better capable of standing the climate than the natives of Madeira, more energetic than the East Indians and less fierce and barbarous than emigrants from the Kroo coast of Africa" (emphasis added).[35]

Cast in the role of middlemen in a sociopolitical buffer zone, the Chinese were depicted as existing in a somewhat blurred space between the ex-slaves and estate management. The Chinese performed substantially the same work and lived under similar conditions as the Black laboring classes, yet colonial texts take care to make a distinction between Blacks and Chinese by regularly portraying the Chinese as being free from the hostile and uncooperative attitudes of some of the Blacks, as well as the Indians, and of being largely supportive of colonial authority, particularly in confrontations between labor and estate management. For example, the 1871 Royal Commission's Report noted with some apparent satisfaction that "[t]he Chinese, as far as we are aware, have never combined with the Indians in disturbances on the estates; but, on the other hand, have occasionally taken the side of the employer in opposing them."[36] On another occasion, Chinese efforts to help quell a confrontation between Black laborers and estate management was positively recognized even though, during that incident, a Black man had been killed.[37]

Although colonial texts differentiated between the Blacks and the Chinese, the latter were never considered to be part of the estate management class to whom they were supposedly so attached. A revealing episode in this regard are the negative descriptions of the Chinese who arrived on the *Corona*, one of the last ships to bring Chinese migrants to Guyana in the nineteenth century. These migrants were strongly criticized for the confidence and curiosity with which they explored their new environment. They wandered about town like tourists, freely entering buildings and examining people and objects with a confidence that was clearly off-putting to the colonials they encountered. The *Royal Gazette* complained that the Chinese had demonstrated a "nonchalance amounting in some cases to positive impertinence" and had exhibited a "patronising air," concluding that obviously the Chinese had mistaken the kindness of the colonials "for inference to themselves as persons of consequence."[38] What is at issue for the colonials is that this group of migrants did not seem to understand its *place* in colonial society; that is, the Chinese did not demonstrate an acceptable level of deference toward the European colonials (the only "persons of consequence" in this society). To ensure that the lower status of the Chinese was made clear, reports on the migrants represented their curiosity as rudeness and their confidence as patronization.

CHIN-A-FOO: LITERARY ANCESTOR OF FICTIONAL CHINESE "WEST INDIANNESS"

Although colonial discourse in official state documents provides some of the context within which more contemporary images of the Chinese would be based, the true literary ancestor of the fictional representations that are at the core of this book is the character Chin-a-foo, who appears in the 1871 novel *Lutchmee and Dilloo.* He is likely the first Chinese character in the fictional landscapes of the West Indies. Chin-a-foo's representation also reveals that the ambiguity with regard to Chinese belonging in the nineteenth-century West Indies was connected to the impact that the Chinese were perceived as having in maintaining plantation economy; that is, the Chinese were imagined as outsiders to the West Indies when their behavior threatened the plantations' survival. The novel was written by

Edward Jenkins, a barrister as well as a satirist of some renown in the nineteenth century, who had been sent to Guyana from England by the Anti-Slavery and Aborigine Protection Societies to represent the indentured immigrants during the Royal Commission's investigation. Jenkins produced two pieces of work from that experience, *The Coolie: His Rights and Wrongs* and a three-volume novel fictionalizing the experience of indentured immigrants, *Lutchmee and Dilloo: A Study of West Indian Life*.

In *Lutchmee and Dilloo*, Jenkins complains that the Chinese are "a hopeless dead-weight to managers and overseers," suggesting that their presence in the West Indies was unnecessary or even dangerous.[39] This negative image of the Chinese is reinforced in the character of Chin-a-foo, where the link between the hostility that Jenkins demonstrates toward the Chinese and the significance of their perceived contribution or lack of contribution to the plantation economy is clear. Chin-a-foo runs a gambling and opium establishment that is depicted as being detrimental to the physical and economic conditions of the other laborers and, by extension, the colony itself. Indeed, Chin-a-foo has so rejected his position as an estate laborer that during slow periods at his gambling den, he chooses to support himself by hunting in the bush rather than working on the estate. In a similar manner, the long description of Chin-a-foo that accompanies his introduction in the text depicts him as physically and morally repulsive. It climaxes with the words, "concealed under the wide paejamas [*sic*], was a knife about two inches broad and fifteen long, tapering to its end, and kept in a state of suspicious brightness."[40] The concealed knife becomes a metaphor for the perceived threat that Chin-a-foo poses to the plantation because of his violent and duplicitous nature that is kept, like his knife, barely under wraps. The ugly depiction of Chin-a-foo is therefore implicated in the fact that Chin-a-foo has rejected his place on the estate. In so doing, Chin-a-foo also rejects his conceptual place in the imaginative landscapes of West Indian colonial discourse and forfeits the possibility of being imagined as a legitimate member—that is, as belonging—in colonial society.

As noted earlier, Chinese acceptance within the colonial landscape had been imagined in terms of their supposed neutralizing effect on revolutionary sentiment. In Jenkins' work, however, both Chin-a-foo and the entire Chinese community are represented as serious threats to estate management. One of the means by which Jenkins does this is by representing the Chinese as being entirely more violent and dangerous than their Indian counterparts. In the melee that occurs when an attempt is made by estate authorities to arrest Chin-a-foo, for example, the Indian participants are depicted as being quickly shamed into orderly behavior and meekly depart the scene. In contrast, the Chinese go back to their quarters where they are described as preparing "for a desperate resistance to the now inevitable visit of the police."[41] Similarly, whenever the novel describes unrest among the indentured laborers, the Indians are always described as having to retrieve their weapons from their homes whereas the Chinese always seem to have their knives with them, possibly, like Chin-a-foo, simply thrust up their sleeves. This subtle distinction effectively emphasizes Jenkins' overall image of the perceived failure of the Chinese community to fulfill the buffer zone role afforded to them in colonial discourse.

Jenkins' work also undermines the status of Chinese belonging in the West Indies by representing the Chinese as not only failing in their neutralizing role but also in actually leaving their middlemen position in the sociopolitical colonial hierarchy to join the ranks of the lower masses. Thus, Jenkins repeatedly depicts the Chinese community as part of a nondescript "coolie strata," as opposed to a community that is distinctly separated from the other groups that make up plantation society, namely, Indian Coolies, Blacks, and estate management. On one occasion, for example, Jenkins suggests that the Chinese are involved in celebrating *Tadja* with the indentured migrants from India. Generally, as with many nineteenth-century West Indian texts, Jenkins distinguishes between "coolies" and "Chinese" in reference to the indentured laborers, reserving the former term for immigrants from India. The Chinese are, however, clearly present at the formal stick fight that occurs during *Tadja* in the novel. Jenkins' description of *Tadja* as a festival in which "*all coolies* join in celebrating" (emphasis added) is therefore significant because the distinction between Chinese and (Indian) coolies becomes blurred.[42] The connection between the Chinese and the Indian communities is even more evident in the chaos that occurs when estate management attempts to arrest Chin-a-foo. In this situation, both the Indians and the Chinese are depicted as fighting side-by-side against Drummond and Craig, the representatives of colonial power and authority. The division is made strikingly clear when Craig is stabbed and a cry goes up from the laborers: "Take him from *them*" (emphasis added).[43] In that short statement, the boundaries delineating the political and social segments of West Indian society are made clear: "us" is the laborers and "them" is estate management. There is, at this point, no middleman between the two groups, for the Chinese have aligned themselves with the Indian "coolies." Faced with uncertainty regarding the actual sociopolitical position that the Chinese would hold in the colony, it is perhaps no surprise that in the end, Jenkins situates Chin-a-foo's gambling establishment on the farthest edges of the estate, bordering the forest. In this way, Chin-a-foo is depicted as belonging neither to the "primitive" forest nor to the "civilized" estate but to an ambiguous nowhere land. In the same way, when the Chinese fail to be seen as protecting the colonial order, their place in the colonies as imagined in colonial discourse becomes blurred and ambiguous.

Jenkins' work and the other nineteenth-century texts briefly reviewed above reveal that the ambiguous portrayal of Chinese belonging articulated the interests of the colonial power. On the one hand, the Chinese were expected through their labor and political neutrality to support colonial interests, and thus could, in this role, be imagined as belonging—as insiders to West Indian spaces. On the other hand, the need to continually affirm White political and sociocultural superiority in the face of the reality that the Chinese did not always fulfill the expectations imagined for them meant that depictions of the Chinese were sometimes very negative, representing them as unwanted additions to the colonies—as outsiders. This ambivalence in terms of affording the Chinese belonging in nineteenth-century ideas of the West Indies reflects what Edward Said describes as the "flexible *positional* superiority" that colonials tried to maintain for themselves as they produced images of the Chinese immigrants.[44] Simply, colonial images of Chinese belonging were flexible—they changed to meet the needs of colonial discourses.

This historical and discursive backdrop plays an important role in the exploration of twentieth-century fictional images of the Chinese in this book. Indeed, many colonial ideas of the Chinese would be revived and reinforced in the subsequent century in the service of nation and national discourses. In particular, this brief historical overview reveals that ideas of Chinese "outsidership" to the postindependent West Indian nations find their roots in the fact that the Chinese were specifically brought into the colonies to reinforce plantation life, as well as in their relatively short period on the plantations as laborers, and their association with colonial power in colonial discourse. This history, along with the high participation of the Chinese in the retail trade sector in the early twentieth century, made it easy for individuals trying to define the nation in both the pre- and the postindependence periods to depict the Chinese as outsiders, exploiters, and enemies of those who were being defined as the nation. But the ambivalence that characterized nineteenth-century depictions of the Chinese is also present in more contemporary fictional depictions of the Chinese. In particular, it does not always suit national narratives to cast the Chinese in the role of oppressor and outsider. Depicting the Chinese as insiders to West Indian spaces by focusing on their shared history and culture with other West Indians, becomes a powerful way of asserting the existence of a unique West Indian cultural identity in a way that mirrors the nineteenth century's use of images of Chinese assimilation to confirm the superiority of the colonial "civilization."

In the subsequent chapters, I explore a spectrum of fictional images that portray Chinese belonging in West Indian literary texts, aiming to illustrate their relationship to the construction of national identities. In Chapter 1, I set out my theoretical approach to examining the literary representation of Chinese in Jamaica, Trinidad, and Guyana. I argue for thinking of nation as the cultural product of *narratives* (rather than *a narrative*). In the case of the West Indies, two narratives are dominant: one that articulates nation in terms of struggle against oppression and the other, in terms of creolization. I also suggest that the idea of national literature be reconceptualized as a site of symbolic performances—albeit banal performances—where various narratives of national identity take place. I argue that the representation of the Chinese is analogous to stock characters in such performances in that they identify which genre of national narrative is being performed. In Chapters 2 and 3, I examine a wide range of West Indian literary texts, exploring how their images of the Chinese situate the Chinese as both outside and inside the imaginative boundaries of nation. I suggest that this ambivalence is characteristic of the fact that nation exists in multiple narratives. Chapter 4 explores how self-representations of Chineseness complicate national narratives of belonging. I pay particular attention to how the diasporic paradigm affects the construction of identity. In the Conclusion, I consider the questions that this research raises for future explorations of nation in general and, more specifically, for the Chinese in the West Indies.

Overall, this book is an exploration into the meaning of "Mr. Chin"—that is, an attempt to read behind the reductive stereotypical images of the Chinese in the West Indies as is perhaps most overtly expressed in the common nickname for Chinese shopkeepers in the West Indies, "Mr Chin." Before we can begin this search for Mr. Chin, however, we would do well to keep in mind a number of caveats. First, there has been little critical interrogation into the literary representations of the Chinese in the West Indies. There lacks, in other words, a strong literary tradition of interrogating "Chineseness" in the West Indies, a situation complicated by the fact that many of the authors studied in this investigation have not reached a high level of international acclaim. Of course, such authors as V. S. Naipaul or Samuel Selvon have generated much critical attention; however, such work does not consider how Chineseness is manifested in their fiction. In contrast, Asian American literary critics have long been dealing with many of the issues that this book addresses. I have therefore placed their work into dialogue with my analysis of Chinese "West Indianness," a decision that I hope will also encourage a more widespread engagement with "Asianness" in the Americas in general. To that end, I also situate this research in comparison with the growing field of research on Chinese experience in Cuba, particularly in light of the fact that both the Chinese Cuban communities and the Chinese communities of the West Indies entered these regions in about the same period and under similar conditions. Finally, despite the somewhat broad regional and chronological scope of this study, I want to emphasize that the experience of the Chinese in the West Indies—indeed in the Caribbean in general—is not homogeneous. Significant differences exist between the experience of the Chinese in Jamaica, Trinidad, and Guyana and in the ways in which nationhood was achieved in all three regions. It is in this sense that I consider this work to be laying the foundation for more specific research into the Chinese of each nation and into "nation-ness" itself. This investigation does, however, provide us with a starting point for searching for Mr. Chin, that is, for considering the cultural impact that the presence of the Chinese has had on the construction of West Indian national identities and, more broadly on a new aspect of Chineseness in the Americas. In doing so, this study situates itself in the "deep and lengthy process of disclosure, one of unfixing entrenched binaries: slave versus free, black versus white, East versus West, Pacific versus Atlantic" with regard to our understanding of Chineseness, Americanness, and West Indianness.[45]

1 / Forgotten Remembrance: Literature and the Banal Performance of Nation

> *Patterns of social life become habitual or routine, and in so doing embody the past. One might describe this process of routine-formation as enhabitation: thoughts, reactions and symbols become turned into routine habits and, thus, they become enhabited. The result is that the past is enhabited in the present in a dialect of forgotten remembrance.*
>
> —MICHAEL BILLIG, *BANAL NATIONALISM*

This book explores the unstable literary representations of Chinese West Indians in relation to imagining them as belonging within West Indian nations and seeks to account for their ambiguous belonging in terms of the articulation of national narratives. Such an investigation requires reconsideration of how the concepts of "nation," "national narrative," and "national identity" are enacted in this region. It also looks at how these ideas affect the relationship between nation and literature. To that end, I would like to *loosely* employ a metaphor of the theater to draw attention to the multiplicity of narratives involved in the performance and imagining of nationhood. In so doing, I want to make a connection between narrative diversity as characteristic of modern constructions of nationhood and the ambiguous representations of belonging for Chinese West Indians.

Academic debate regarding the "nation" often begins with a distinction between the (nation-)state and the nation.[1] The state is described as a clearly defined political territory (it has a government) that is recognized as distinct by the populations within and without the geographical boundaries of that territory. In contrast, the nation is defined as a population that believes or imagines that it is a group that somehow belongs together on the grounds of a distinct shared history, often understood to encompass a shared bloodline, cultural practices and/or values, or some combination of the three. These specific commonalities are understood to be the defining features of the nation and thus its national identity. A state and a nation are therefore not necessarily the same thing—indeed, by such a definition, multiple nations might exist within a state. However, it is understood that nations generally seek their own state; that is, they seek to control a specific geographical territory where political policies are enacted by and on behalf of the nation. As such, nationalism is often defined as those activities that the nation utilizes in the attempt to gain its own state, although it can also be more broadly understood to include the various activities by which a nation asserts itself or its identity, whether or not in the pursuit of statehood. The production of a nation can therefore be understood to be both an act of political assertion and "a form of cultural elaboration."[2]

In "On National Culture," Frantz Fanon argued for the centrality of culture to the production of the nation when he posited that "the conscious and organized undertaking by a colonized people to re-establish the sovereignty of that nation constitutes the most complete and obvious cultural manifestation that exists."[3] Although Fanon was specifically considering the experience of postcolonial nations like Jamaica, Trinidad, and Guyana, culture—both in the sense of artistic productions and as shared patterns of behavior, norms, and values—has long been understood to play a significant role in the creation of modern nations. Culture's ability to be both a vehicle for expressing the ideas, images, and myths in which the collective identities of nation are grounded and a form of expression that necessitates and creates bonds between members of a community makes it a significant means by which to justify and to understand the sociopolitical form that we know as the nation. Thus, Fanon suggests that one can trace the development of national consciousness in colonized nations through the themes that appear in their literature;

Ernest Gellner argues that universal education disseminates a shared system of cultural norms and values that serve as the precondition for inventing the nation; and Benedict Anderson locates the roots of nationalism in the cultural practice of language. Homi K. Bhabha also prioritizes the role of culture in the creation of nations when he argues that nations "come into being" through narrative, that is, a "system of cultural signification."[4] Timothy Brennan makes a similar claim when he suggests that the literary text is particularly implicated within this system of signification and is therefore an appropriate site from which to consider nationhood.

> The rise of the modern nation-state in Europe in the late eighteenth and early nineteenth centuries is inseparable from the forms and subjects of imaginative literature. On the one hand, the political tasks of modern nationalism directed the course of literature, leading through the Romantic concepts of "folk character" and "national language" to the (largely illusory) divisions of literature into distinct "national literatures." On the other hand, and just as fundamentally, literature participated in the formation of nations through the creation of "national print media"—the newspaper and the novel. . . . [I]t was especially the novel as a composite but clearly bordered work of art that was crucial in defining the nation as an "imagined community."[5]

National narratives can be defined as "those traditions of political thought and literary language" that create what Ernest Renan described as "large-scale solidarity" among the populace who comes to see themselves as a nation—a community that imagines that it belongs together.[6] In other words, it is through narrative that nations set out their cultural boundaries of belonging. Ironically, however, as the act of narrating reveals "tension between the pedagogical and the performative" aspects of narration, it is in the very pursuit of solidarity through narrative that these boundaries become unstable and belonging has the potential to be represented in an ambivalent manner.[7]

For Bhabha, the ambiguity of nation as a cultural construct is connected to the fact that he locates nation in "double-time"—a blurred spatial temporality between a mythic past and the actual lived experience of nation that is made evident by the "continual slippage into analogous, even metonymic, categories like the people, minorities, or 'cultural difference' that continually overlap in the act of writing the nation."[8] A nation legitimizes its existence on the basis of a mythic past that, in turn, must correspond with the everyday lived reality that the nation experiences in the present. In other words, the "current-time nation" must match the "timeless nation" if either nation is to exist. Bhabha argues that ambiguity occurs within national narratives because the images in which they are constructed must negotiate between the present and the past in such a fashion that the present is always being collapsed into the past. Thus, Bhabha concludes that the "language of culture and community is poised on the fissures of the present becoming the rhetorical figures of a national past."[9]

It is not, however, simply the process of narrating in this blurred time zone (so to speak), which turns nation into "an agency of ambivalent narration."[10] The ambivalent representation of belonging is also the result of the narrative's content. The narrative reveals, in other words, the choices that are made to include or exclude events, people and perspectives in the creation of a cohesive national "story." These choices are what allow the national self to imagine that it has "common glories in the past and . . . a common will in the present."[11] These "foundational fictions" require an act of will that Renan described as "forgetting."[12] As Regina Lee puts it, "Commonality . . . legitimizes the nation-state's claim to homogeneity, leads to the imagination and idealization of a pure, unified self. The Other (impure) voices that make up the nation-state get obscured, forgotten, or silenced—in other words, excluded."[13] While they may be marginalized, these Others do not, however, disappear. Instead, Bhabha insists that their presence "haunts the idea of the nation."[14] In doing so, they force open a conceptual space in the national narrative in which the representation of the nation can be contested and even displaced. More specifically, the existence of those identified as not belonging within the nation interrupts the narrative authority on which the nation is established, which, in turn, undermines the authoritative closure on which the pedagogical image of nation is based. Thus, nation and the boundaries of belonging that it attempts to establish are rendered ambiguous, and national narrative becomes but an "*attempt* at self-mythologizing" (emphasis added) and a site of "incomplete signification."[15]

The ambiguity of the concept of nation that interests theorists such as Bhabha is rooted in the artifice of homogeneity that emerges in the narration of nation. Therefore, the intent of their analyses is, to reinvoke Renan, to remember difference, to remember that which is attempted to be forgotten in the process of narrating the nation and to explore the processes that allow or encourage such forgetting. The implication of such study is that the pursuit of national cohesiveness requires the creation of *one* narrative. There may be a number of "foundational fictions," but ultimately they are understood to work together to create one "grand narrative of the nation-state."[16] After all, an understanding of nation as being haunted and a system of "incomplete signification," as articulated by Bhabha, is premised on the existence of other counternarratives that threaten the grand narrative's ability to imagine a unified national self. That such narratives are deemed to exist in antagonistic tension with each other, or at least with the nation's grand narrative, is suggested in the term "counternarrative": a narrative that sets itself up *against* another narrative. Thus, the analysis of the ambiguity in the concept of nation has traditionally captured the "ongoing desire for an 'imagined community' undercut by the very conditions of its enunciation."[17]

This book, however, begins from a slightly different premise. It takes as a given that the "discontinuities endemic to modern life and the inescapably plural character of modern identity" are applicable to the nation as well as to individuals, such that multiple national narratives must not only exist but also can be seen as indicative of a nation's modernity; further, the existence of such narrative diversity need not be conceived in terms of antagonism and opposition as is suggested in the idea of a counternarrative.[18] Instead, it is possible that such narratives, despite establishing different boundaries of belonging, simply coexist, that they are merely "*other* narratives" rather than *counter*narratives. Accepting such a premise allows us to link the ambiguity noted in the articulation of national belonging to the existence of diverse narratives that "coarticulate" multiple ways of imagining the nation.

The study of West Indian literature to further understanding of the relationship between ambiguous representations of national belonging and modernity is particularly appropriate because the distinctive characteristics of modern societies existed in the plantation colonies of the West Indies from the earliest times of European contact. From an economic standpoint, these include the presence of a capitalist socioeconomic culture based on mass production and consumption of goods, the ownership of private property, and an investment in industrialization and technology. Socially, modern societies are noted for having class divisions that correspond to divisions of labor and particularly multiethnic populations (due to the economic organization of the society) who produce vibrant, cultural hybridity. Both social characteristics were present very early in the West Indies. Major philosophies and ideologies associated with modernity, along with their accompanying discursive tensions and contradictions, can also be discerned in the West Indies, such as the belief in human progress that was supported through historical and scientific discourses and the construction of a European identity formed in contrast to that of a racialized "Other." In fact, in support of the claim that the West Indies are "the primordial site of Atlantic modernity," the historian Hilary Beckles picturesquely summed up West Indian modernity by describing it as the "invisible cargo" that Columbus brought with him to the region, which included

> an economic ideology which was not yet labeled nor understood, but which came to be understood as something called commercial capitalism; the ideology of racism which at that time was not clearly articulated, but which rooted itself in the Caribbean; the social ideology of patriarchy which assumed the superior political and intellectual capacity of men over women; an intolerant Christian theology which defined other religions as primitive subtypes; an expansionist imperialist consciousness that focused on total territorial acquisition; and a rationalist philosophy that promoted the notion of materialism as the way forward for mankind.[19]

The impact of Western-style modernity such as that experienced in the West Indies on the creation of dynamic and fluid national identities can be seen in what social scientists have observed as the tension between ethnicized and civic-based articulations of modern nationhood as expressed in narrative. Theorists, such as Gellner, who define nations in terms of civic-based communities argue that the nation is imagined as a political entity that was developed in response to the new political and economic conditions of modernity. The civic-based idea of nation locates belonging within shared civic values, goals, and mutual responsibilities among the citizenry. The focus on civic values and responsibilities around which such ideas of nation are formulated tends to be somewhat nebulous and nonspecific. As such, they are generally attributes that can be attained by a broad spectrum of individuals despite the presence of cultural or ethnic differences. For example, one might speak a different dialect or language at home yet can also communicate in the official language of the state. Nations founded on the idea of a civic-based community thus allow for somewhat inclusive boundaries to mark out belonging. In particular, ethnic difference can be accommodated as long as it does not interfere with the overarching civic values and responsibilities expressed in the state culture. Ethnic-based ideas of nation are, by contrast, much less flexible in their designation of who can belong to the nation.

Anthropologists use the term "ethnicity" to indicate boundaries between population groups who consider themselves to be culturally distinct from others. These distinctions, identified by Manning Nash as "blood, substance and deity," basically encompass ideas of a shared biological descent, usually attached to a specific homeland and a shared history, a common name for the group, and a common value system, often expressed in religious terms.[20] It is the sense of consanguinity—the understanding that the nation is a "family group"—that is central to this concept of nation and is the source of its powerful appeal. It is also the foundation for its exclusive boundaries, for one can only be a part of the nation by bloodline—if one is "born into" it. The group members' distinctive physical and cultural traits become important reference points for designating who can or cannot belong to the nation. Thus, ethnic differences become useful as boundary markers that define the national community.

Rather than conceiving of nations as constructing identities solely in terms of civic or ethnic narratives, it has been recognized that the modern nation "has come to blend two sets of dimensions, the one civic and territorial, the other ethnic and genealogical in varying proportions" rendering the nation's boundaries of belonging "problematic and uncertain."[21] This is particularly true of ex-colonies, like those of the former British West Indies, who faced the task of imagining community and belonging for diverse multiethnic populations when they achieved independence in the mid-twentieth century. An examination of the national narratives that emerged from this region around the time of independence reveals a continued shifting between two ways of conceiving belonging, one that prioritizes ethnic commonality and another that validates a more fluid sense of identity. It is these imaginative shifts that point to the existence of unfixed and multiple national narratives.

Anthony D. Smith argues that most ex-colonies construct their national identities on a "supra-ethnic" model; that is, nationalists make a conscious effort not to prioritize any ethnic group within the nation, choosing instead to base images of group solidarity and community on common civic values, political ambitions, and experiences. The national symbols produced in Jamaica, Trinidad, and Guyana demonstrate such broad definitions of national boundaries. For example, the color schemes of their national flags are meant to be visual representations of the qualities and values considered representative of their nations' citizenry, such as courage, vitality, and perseverance, none of which can be deemed "ethnic-specific." Similarly, the national anthems of each region identify their citizens—those who belong—as individuals who commit their lives and service to the nation and its other citizens, with Trinidad's anthem making the most explicit claim to nonethnic inclusivity in its declaration that "here every creed and race find an equal place." Their national mottoes also seek to depict an image of a united people whose sense of national community marginalizes ethnic differences. Thus, Guyana describes itself as "one people, one nation, one destiny"; Trinidad asserts that "together we aspire; together we achieve"; and Jamaica proclaims, "out of many, one people."

In more "lived" or everyday articulations of nationhood, however, the nation's boundaries are often situated within a narrative of oppression, and resistance to said oppression, that is linked directly to the experience of slavery. In this way, national belonging is grounded in the more ethnically specific community of slaves and their descendants. This tendency away from "supra-ethnicity" is apparent in the manner in which leading nationalists of the independence period described their nations in their public appearances and speeches. In Jamaica, for example, Norman Manley defined the People's National Party as the defender of the "little man," namely the predominantly Black peasant farmer or laborer, declaring that the "objective of government . . . is the improvement of the conditions under which ordinary people live" and that "the mass of the population [that is, Blacks] are the *real people*. . . . [T]hose who will not unite with them on all fundamentals are the real *aliens in the land*" (emphasis added).[22] Similarly, in Guyana, Cheddi Jagan often foregrounded the experiences of slavery as being the crucible in which Guyanese nationhood would be formed by characterizing indenture as another manifestation of slavery—that is, as a process by which "paper chains were substituted for iron chains"—in his nationalist rhetoric.[23]

In Trinidad, the so-called Chaguaramas Incident also revealed the subtle prioritization of the slave experience in national narrative when Eric Williams attempted to arouse support for protests against the continued American occupation at Chaguaramas. In a speech to protesters, Williams made the following rallying call:

> Our enemies said we would never be free. They said we would never be fit for freedom. They said we could never govern ourselves. They said that we were a lazy, servile race, desirous only of sitting in the sun and eating yams and pumpkins, capable only of aping the graces of our European masters. They said we could never operate democratic institutions, we could never be governed along European lines. Our magnificent demonstration today gives the lie to this imperialist indictment of the West Indian people.[24]

On the surface, "the West Indian people" of Williams' speech seems to refer to any Trinidadian who had lived within the colonial period regardless of ethnic background; however, the allusion around which Williams builds his speech is actually much more specific. He draws directly on popular nineteenth-century images of the slaves and ex-slaves lying around and eating yams that were propagated by anti-abolitionist writers of that period such as Anthony Trollope and Thomas Carlyle.[25] By choosing this narrow reference point, Williams' definition of "West Indian people" actually focuses on slaves and those who directly inherited the legacy of slavery. The preciseness of his allusion makes it difficult to incorporate other experiences into his vision of national community. Thus, the national narrative that defines nationhood in a story of oppression and resistance converges with the boundaries of an ethnic community—those individuals who were descended from African slaves—creating a much more exclusive boundary to national belonging.

Despite locating the nation in slavery, Williams is also well remembered for making the following dramatic claim for ethnic inclusivity in the nation:

> There can be no Mother India for those whose ancestors came from India. . . .There can be no Mother Africa for those of African origin. . . .There can be no Mother England. . . .There can be no Mother China . . . no Mother Syria or no Mother Lebanon. A nation, like an individual, can have only one Mother. The only Mother we recognize is Mother Trinidad and Tobago, and Mother cannot discriminate between her children. All must be equal in her eyes.[26]

It is this switching between inclusive and exclusive national narratives that is apparent in the political articulations of nation that I am interested in tracing when I ask, how do the fictional representations of the Chinese contribute to understanding how national narratives in the West Indies are created and maintained? To engage in such a study, however, requires a broad survey of West Indian literature and an equally broad definition of national literature. As such, I want to move away from the common, yet narrow practice of defining "national literature" as that which is concerned with overtly asserting national identity in the pursuit of statehood. Fanon's definition of national literature is typical in this regard.

> [National literature takes up and clarifies] themes which are typically nationalist. . . . [It is] a literature of combat, in the sense that it calls on the whole people to fight for their existence as a nation. It is a literature of combat, because it molds the national consciousness . . . because it assumes responsibility, and because it is the will to liberty expressed in terms of time and space.[27]

In contrast, I want to think of nationalism, and by extension, national literature, as having a wider scope; specifically, I want to think of nationalism as the imaginative condition within which literature, particularly the type of realistic fiction typical of the West Indies, is produced, regardless of whether or not national ambition is acknowledged within the literary text. This approach suggests that we recognize that the cultural construct of nation remains the backdrop, albeit unacknowledged, within which the text's story takes place; further, that rather than considering literature to be "national" only when nation-ness is presented in an overtly political fashion, this often unconscious framing of fiction within nation space can provide significant insight into the implicit everyday ways in which nationhood and national belonging are acted out. To that end, I posit that for this study, the relationship between nation and literature be understood within the terms of what Michael Billig describes as "banal nationalism."

Billig argues that nationalism is not only a political movement aimed exclusively at establishing nation-states; nationalism also exists in a quiet, yet persistent form in established Western nations where its aim is to maintain, rather than create, a nation-state. Billig notes that the nation forms the ideological backdrop against and within which individuals exist regardless of whether or not a concern with nationhood is explicitly identified. He also locates the habits of everyday social life as sites of national identity. Within this ideological expression of nation, he defines national identity as consisting of "forms of a social life rather than internal psychological states."[28] In fact, Billig suggests that the power of nation lies in the implicit ways in which it is continually reproduced in everyday practices that remind citizens that they live within a specific nation that is itself located in a world of nations. These practices are what Billig calls "flagging the nation" and include such behavior as speaking of the national news or international sports competitions where the unspoken idea of nation is the only context within which such statements make any sense. Thus, Billig concludes that nationalism, "far from being an intermittent mood in established nations, is the endemic condition" and coins the phrase "banal nationalism" to describe this phenomenon.[29] It is on this conception of nation as "the endemic condition" of lived experience that is reproduced in realistic fiction that I ground my contention that the wide variety of West Indian literature under investigation in this book be considered "national literature"—literature that actively participates in the articulation of nationhood even if only as a backdrop to the text.

I want to be careful to clarify that in using this broad definition of national literature I am not suggesting that the fiction considered in this book be read as national allegory in the way in which critics such as Aijaz Ahmad interpreted Fredric Jameson's now infamous claim that "[a]ll third-world texts . . . are to be read as . . . *national allegories*."[30] The widespread negative response among literary theorists to Jameson's argument was centered not only on a rejection of what some perceived to be his reification of the Three Worlds theory and homogenizing reduction of the complex experiences and histories of the so-called Third World, but on an oversimplified distinction between "Third World" and "First World" writing resulting from the employment of an allegorical model for analysis. In particular, they contested the limiting possibilities for what might be the content of "Third World" literature and the literary analysis of such texts that seemed the natural result of Jameson's assertion:

> [O]ne of the determinants of capitalist culture, that is, the culture of the western realist and modernist novel, is a radical split between the private and the public, between the poetic and the political. . . . Third-world texts . . . necessarily project a political dimension in the form of national allegory: the story of the private individual destiny is always an allegory of the embattled situation of the public third-world culture and society.[31]

As Ahmad put it in his well-known response to Jameson:

> If this "Third World" is constituted by the singular "experi-

> ence of colonialism and imperialism," and if the only possible response is a nationalist one, then what else is there that is more urgent to narrate than this "experience"? In fact, there is nothing else to narrate.[32]

In the 2008 article "A Caribbean Response to the Question of Third World National Allegories: Jameson, Ahmad and the Return of the Repressed," however, Roberto Strongman challenges the presumed negative implications of having "nothing else to narrate" by situating West Indian writing firmly within its political and historical context. He argues that reading West Indian literature as national allegory is actually an act of empowerment rather than a sign of the literature's primitive or less artistically matured status, a fear that Ahmad evokes in his own rejection of the national allegory as indicative of "Third World" writing. Instead, Strongman presents a compelling argument for understanding national allegory as a powerful means by which authors resist the historical denial of West Indian subjectivity that was the legacy of the plantation experience. In doing so, however, Strongman also inadvertently points to one of the reasons I hesitate to read the depictions of Chineseness in West Indian literature within a national allegorical framework.

Strongman's analysis is based on limiting his literary field of investigation to West Indian coming-of-age stories, which are read as allegorical of the nation's developing political maturity. My approach to this study follows Edward Said in that it seeks to analyze "the relationship between texts and the way in which groups of texts, types of texts, even textual genres, acquire mass density, and referential power among themselves and thereafter in the culture at large."[33] Nevertheless, my subject of investigation focuses on a community in the West Indies that is a minority both literally and imaginatively. There is very little fiction from the West Indies that centers on Chinese West Indians. As a result, much of my analysis considers the representation of minor literary characters. I simply, therefore, cannot afford to be limited to texts that are overt political allegories in my consideration of West Indian Chineseness as this would render a small field of investigation even narrower than it already is. Further, the relationship between allegory and meaning-making occurs on a one-to-one basis. What is represented in the allegorical story has one clear allegorical meaning. A character in an allegory named Faith, for example, would hardly be expected to display any other qualities than that determined by her name. To approach West Indian literature as "an allegory of the embattled situation of the public third-world culture and society" suggests not only an overdetermination of the national narrative that might emerge from such an analysis; it also implies that there is *one narrative construct,* that is, one political story that is being allegorized. Such an approach directly counters my interest in the existence of narrative multiplicity that the ambiguous fictional representations of Chinese belonging suggest. I seek a more nuanced analysis of the relationship between the political and personal sphere in terms of setting the boundaries of nation that can be gleaned by reading the texts as a "representation of social *life* rather than the discipline of social *polity.*"[34] My focus is, therefore, on the subtle interactions and exchanges between a nation's community members in its representations of Chinese West Indians. I read the repetitive images of such interactions as a type of stylized gesture that creates and conveys meaningful understandings of West Indian nationhood. As such, for my purposes, the idea of performance, rather than allegory, provides a better means of accessing the texts under study. It is in this sense that a metaphor of the theater, in its vaguest of forms, is an apt analogy by which to think through the ambiguous representations of Chineseness in West Indian literature.

The way in which gendered identities gain meaning and are "naturalized" through what Judith Butler famously described as the repeated performance of stylized gestures gives us a framework for thinking of identity as a cultural performance. Butler argues that "the various ways in which a body shows or produces its cultural signification, are performative."[35] This type of cultural performance is best understood as "the social process by which actors, individually or in concert, display for others the meaning of their social situation."[36] Thus, the performance of identity is a means of establishing a "banalized knowledge"; that is, it consists of "the everyday practices through which social actors produce aesthetic values, ideological perspectives, and gender, race, class, national and sexual identities."[37]

In breaking down the constituent parts of a performance, theorists of drama also provide a model for understanding how the literary text can be read as a cultural performance of nationhood. The traditional model of performance involves the actors; an audience; a site from which the performance occurs; matrices of collective systems of representation, such as narrative, that condense and elaborate "social and emotional life in compelling and coherent ways" (also known as "the context"); and the actual "gestures that constitute performance."[38] In exploring representations of Chinese West Indianness as the performance of national belonging, I want to think of national literature, that is, the whole body of literature produced by a nation, as a stage—the site from which the performance of national identity occurs for a reading public (the audience) both within and without the nation-state. The interactions between fictional characters (the actors), particularly the exchanges between Chinese and non-Chinese characters in individual pieces of fiction, are the stylized gestures by which belonging is performed. The context or the collective system of representation against which the performance gains meaning is either the civic- or ethnic-based national narrative. In other words, the repeated images of the Chinese in West Indian literary texts can be read as stylized representations or gestures of belonging that give concrete meaning to the more abstract ideas of national community that are articulated in national narratives. Thus, the performance of Chineseness overlaps with the performance of nation such that it makes "tangible that which might otherwise be impossible to meaningfully apprehend, and [brings] a sense of concreteness to the highly abstract"—for an audience that consists of both the reader and the characters in the text themselves.[39]

My use of the theater as a framework through which to explore the ambiguity of West Indian national belonging as expressed in narrative is also motivated by other theoretical considerations. Specifically, by considering national literature as a stage from which belonging is performed, I also seek to disrupt the tendency to assert that nations are defined by one grand, albeit, fragmented narrative. Just as any number of plays can be produced on any one stage, I contend that any number of narratives of national belonging can be performed in literature. The ambiguous national belonging evidenced in the various representations of Chineseness that occurs in West Indian literature is therefore a revelation of a diversity of performances on the national stage. Additionally, the theater analogy also permits one to think of national narratives as being organized by genres in much the same way that plays can be organized. In particular, we can imagine ethnic- and civic-based national narratives as being two specific genres in terms of articulating the boundaries of the national community. Thus the fictional representation of the Chinese can be read as analogous to stock characters in terms of identifying which genre of national narrative forms the banal backdrop to the performance of nation.

In many ways, the ambiguous textual representations of the Chinese produced in the West Indies that form the focus of this book become the boundaries of the nation itself. Inclusive images of the Chinese indicate that the imaginative boundary of belonging has been grounded in a civic understanding of nation, whereas images of the Chinese as aliens or outsiders point to a more ethnically specific boundary. In the subsequent chapters I explore both uses of Chineseness. Chapter 2 examines how images of the Chinese are used to dramatize a separation between those accorded valid membership in the new nations and those who, although they exist within the physical borders of the nation, are nonetheless considered outsiders to the national community. In Chapter 3, I explore the links between the representation of the Chinese as insiders to the nation and important contributors to the process of creating a national identity with the pressure to demonstrate the existence of a distinct local culture that accompanies any claim to nationhood. The ways in which Chinese West Indians complicate both of these traditional uses of Chineseness are examined in Chapter 4.

It has been asked whether it is possible to "explain how the integration of particular groups and sometimes even whole collectivities can be achieved through symbolic communications, while continuing to account for cultural complexity and contradiction, for institutional differentiation, contending social power and segmentation."[40] As ritualistically performed gestures of belonging, the textual representations of the Chinese explored in this book provide a partial answer to that challenge. These images provide a symbolic means of consolidating a collective sense of identity in communities that are significantly ethnically diverse. Such imagery is however, highly inconsistent and even, at times, contradictory. Within these inconsistencies, the cultural complexities of modern societies are revealed, particularly in terms of establishing the imaginative boundaries of nation. Indeed, the idea of nation itself is revealed to never be absolute or permanent. By recognizing the artificiality of national boundaries as a cultural construct, images of the Chinese in the West Indies have much to contribute to our understanding of the complexity involved in the performance of nation.

2 / "Just Another Chinaman": The Chinese as Outsiders to the Nation

... at a time like this he is just another Chinaman.

—V. S. NAIPAUL, *GUERRILLAS*

Edward Said opens *Orientalism* with the claim that "Americans will not feel quite the same about the Orient" as Europeans.[1] He does so partially in recognition of the very different contact history that the United States has had with "the Orient" in comparison with that of Britain or France. Said notes that even the definition of "the Orient" has different connotations for Americans than it has for Europeans. He suggests that for Americans "the Orient" tends to denote what Said describes as the "Far East," namely China and Japan, rather than including areas commonly designated as the "Middle East" (what Said calls the "Near East"). Said makes these distinctions as part of his well-known assertion that "the Orient has helped to define Europe" as a counterimage.[2] But his implication that the Orient—particularly the "Far East"—has not played a significant role in the way that North America defines itself is somewhat premature. Indeed, Asian American scholars have long demonstrated that the presence of "the Oriental" on American soil has been a significant foil against which "Americanness" has been conceived. As Lisa Lowe put it, "In the last century and a half, the American *citizen* has been defined over against the Asian *immigrant*, legally, economically, and culturally."[3]

Lowe is interested in legally sanctioned definitions of national belonging as enacted through citizenship; however, she is also quick to note that such definitions find their validity in cultural expression.

> Although the law is perhaps the discourse that most literally governs citizenship, U.S. national culture—the collectively forged images, histories and narratives that place, displace and replace individuals in relation to the national polity—powerfully shapes who the citizenry is, where they dwell, what they remember, and what they forget. . . . The differentiation of Asian immigrants from the national citizenry is marked not only politically but culturally as well: refracted through images, memories, and narratives—submerged, fragmented, and sedimented in a historical "unconscious."[4]

Lowe's exploration into the ways in which the law and popular culture are complicit in the process of orientalizing Asians in the United States finds particular resonance in the study of American literature. Indeed, perhaps unsurprisingly, as Asian American authors and literary critics such as Maxine Hong Kingston and Frank Chin were at the vanguard of the movement to establish Asian American Studies in the United States in the 1960s and 1970s, there is a large body of scholarship that explores the racialized literary depictions of Asians and Asian Americans from their earliest nineteenth-century manifestations, including "John Chinaman" and the "Heathen Chinee," to more contemporary representations. A major strand of research in this area has been to demonstrate how "Asianness" has been inscribed as "Otherness" in America by means of such repetitive stereotypes as the emasculated Asian male or the hypersexualized Asian female. Elaine Kim's conclusion that American literary depictions of Asians have traditionally existed "to define the white man's virility and the white race's superiority" provides a succinct summary of the findings in this field.[5] They also reflect Said's own conclusion that Orientalism "is never far from . . . the idea of European identity as a superior one in comparison with all the non-European peoples and cultures" such that cultural representations of Asians in the United States converge with political discourses and practices to create a type of American "Asianism" that holds much the same role in its national narratives that Said afforded to "the Orient" for Europe: "one of its deepest and most recurring images of the Other . . . its contrasting image, ideal personality, experience . . .[such that t]he Orient is an integral part of [American] *material* civilization and culture."[6]

Unlike Asian American literary critique, Orientalist readings regarding representations of Chineseness in the West Indies are largely nonexistent, the specific concern with Orientalism often being subsumed under more general postcolonial analyses of literary texts. Indeed, in terms of even considering fictional depictions of the Chinese in these regions, Joyce Johnson's 1997 article "Representations of the Chinese in Anglophone Caribbean Fiction" stands out as the first (and for a long time, only) real attempt to provide a sustained engagement with Chineseness in this region. In the greater Caribbean, however, a growing body of scholarship on the representations of the Chinese in Latin American literary texts, especially Cuba, is emerging. The work of literary scholars such as Lancelot Cowie, Julia Kushigian, and Ignacio López-Calvo not only suggests "the importance of this ethnic group in the [Latin American] imaginary" but also reveals some of the striking ways in which Orientalist strategies of representation (generally of the Chinese) are renegotiated.[7] Kushigian's exploration of how "the Orient" functions in the imaginaries of Argentinean Jorge Luis Borges, Mexican Octavio Paz, and Cuban Servero Sarduy concludes that Latin American Orientalism differs significantly from its European counterpart in terms of a perceived greater flexibility of the relationship and distance between East and West, which she suggests is actually a blending, rather than distancing, of opposites.[8] The result is an emphasis on romanticized and exoticized images of "the Orient" in such work. In his study on Chinese representations in Cuba, however, López-Calvo warns that "there are also numerous examples of a less 'respectful' and 'venerating' approach to the Chinese and their culture" evident in the region, flushing out both Sinophobic and negative Orientalist depictions of the Chinese in a broad cross section of literary texts in his work.[9] Cowie also finds a similar attitude demonstrated toward the Chinese as revealed in the conclusion to his own research into Cuban Chinese fictional representations: "Neither the short story writers nor the novelists explore the psychology of the Chinese. Instead, they offer short glimpses of the life of the Oriental in certain prescribed situations. As a result, the characters are somewhat diluted (by their new environment) and operate in the narrative like wretched puppets."[10]

In the West Indies, fictional representations of the Chinese have traditionally been heavily invested in their depiction as an alien presence in the region; and, identified as aliens, the Chinese become the contrasting image for establishing those who are deemed to belong in the nation. What generally defines Chinese alienation in West Indian literary texts is the representation of a financial, political, and sociocultural division of interests. These texts either pit the Chinese directly against other West Indians or position them as aloof, unaffected, and/or entirely distanced from the stresses and difficulties that other West Indians encounter. Taken together, these repetitive images of West Indians struggling against the Chinese, or struggling against forces that do not impact the Chinese, become ritualized as a means of performing a narrative of West Indianness that is located within resistance to oppression and exploitation.

Predators and Parasites

Images of virility and manhood are central to the self-image that national and postcolonial discourses construct in the West Indies. Such images stand in direct contrast to colonial discourses' common presentations of the colonized "Other" as childish or brutish—imagery that had been employed as part of the colonizers' claim to a right and a responsibility to dominate the colonized. Throughout twentieth-century West Indian texts, alternative images assert the independence of the former colonized people and their ability to manage their own affairs, particularly through images of capable manhood, where manhood is often measured by economic success and sexual prowess.[11] What happens, however, when the image of effective independent manhood comes into contact with the often overwhelming difficulties West Indians face in their attempts to dismantle the economic structures that ensured limited access to colonial power and privilege in their postcolonial milieus? The result is that measures of manhood, particularly on an economic level, are often unavailable to the average West Indian in his daily life. In the face of this reality, a common stereotype of the Chinese to emerge in the twentieth century is that of a financial and sexual threat to the very sense of independent selfhood that national discourses in the West Indies struggle to maintain and assert.

In the masculine world of V. S. Naipaul's *Miguel Street*, viable manhood is closely identified with both economic and sexual successes. Indeed, since economic success is generally absent from the lives of the characters, sexual virility becomes the more common signifier of manhood in the text. Thus, tiny Mr. Morgan points to the fact that he has fathered ten children as the key reason that he should be accepted into the street's clique, while Hat notes that Bogart is only able to "be a man, among we men," once he has had children—even though he has to commit bigamy to do so.[12] Eddoes' situation is slightly different in that his manhood is built on some relative economic success and the accumulation of status symbols, both of which are, however, connected to his work as a garbage man. This situation, combined with the powerful effects that an unnamed Chinese man has on his life, demonstrates that Eddoes' manhood is, like the garbage he collects, actually a "cast-off" of those who had power under the colonial regime (and, in this story, still retain power despite the changing times). Within this power structure, the Chinese are represented as being a part of the configuration of oppression.

The fragility of Eddoes' claim to manhood is demonstrated in how easily it is threatened. This occurs when a woman claims that he is the father of her unborn child, even though it is revealed later in the story that paternity belongs to a Chinese man. As the child's father, this unnamed and never seen Chinese man nonetheless endangers all the symbols of Eddoes' manhood. On the most obvious level, Eddoes has failed sexually to prove himself a man; he has not actually produced a child. More tangentially, yet perhaps even more importantly, by impregnating the woman, this Chinese man has not only undermined Eddoes sexually, he also puts Eddoes' job at risk—for the woman claims that she will have Eddoes fired if he does not take financial responsibility for raising the baby. In the end, although the community on the street symbolically gives Eddoes back his manhood by accepting the baby as his own despite its obvious Chinese phenotype, the impact of the Chinese man on Eddoes' life reveals the hollowness of Eddoes' claims to manhood. As such, the story makes both the reader and the community on the street aware of the real powerlessness of Eddoes, for he cannot truly claim his job, his junk, or his daughter as his own.[13]

The image of the Chinese as a sexual threat to the national community that appears in *Miguel Street* is often repeated in the representation of the relationship between the male Chinese shopkeeper and village women in other literary texts. The Chinese shopkeeper is commonly portrayed as a sexual predator who preys on the financial vulnerability of the women. This is certainly suggested in Alfred Mendes' short story "Her Chinaman's Way," when Maria becomes involved with Wing simply because such a relationship seems to offer a way out of her dire financial predicament; or in "Jakes Makes," by Alecia McKenzie, when Grace, who has consistently rejected the attentions of all the "near dead" Black men in the village, suddenly turns up pregnant by her boss, the old Mr. Chang.[14] The relationship between the Chinaman and Zuela in *Bruised Hibiscus*, by Elizabeth Nunez, and Chin-Quee and Martha in *The Hills of Hebron*, by Sylvia Wynter, are also represented in the most repulsive terms.[15] The Chinaman is essentially a rapist, and perhaps also a pedophile, and Chin-Quee is described as a brutalizing machine during his sexual liaisons with Martha. Indeed, for Martha their overall relationship is specifically described as slavery.

In Samuel Selvon's *A Brighter Sun*, this undercurrent of danger that the Chinese shopkeepers pose appears in the relationship that Tall Boy has with the village women despite Selvon's attempts to reduce Tall Boy's behavior to the level of a joke. Tall Boy is depicted as possessing some power over the village women and, by extension, their men because he is permitted to make sexual jokes and touch the women in a way that would clearly never be allowed by any other man. The link between economic power and sexual exploitation evident in these relationships lies in the fact that the Chinese shopkeeper has the power to deny goods and services to those who displease him. Thus, although Tall Boy is deemed "harmless" by the village men, his ability to deny groceries to those who dare to complain about his behavior suggests an alternative understanding of the villagers' tolerance of Tall Boy's harassment in the paragraph's closing lines.

> Tall Boy made fun with all the girls and young women in the village, even when Mary [his wife] was present. She never paid attention to him laughing and leaning over the counter to touch their bodies. He told them, smiling, that he was going to sleep with them that night and they said, "But Tall Boy too fresh, oui! Yuh too fast wid yuhself!" When Mary was in the parlour he held their hands or commented on their figures, in the bar he said to the men, "That is ah good one to sleep wid!" and the men laughed because they knew he was harmless. If the girls got angry he asked them if they couldn't take a joke. "Dou-dou, yuh know is only a joke Ah making. Come, wat it is yuh want, butter? No butter dis week. No saltfish either."[16]

The economic power imbalance that translates to sexual vulnerability for the women is even more explicit in *Bruised Hibiscus* when Zuela, learning that the Chinaman has exposed their son to opium, finally stands up to the Chinaman, threatening to "make a hell" for him by depriving him of both sex and opium.[17] The Chinaman recognizes that Zuela is actually threatening his life; and, although physically and emotionally weakened by years of opium abuse and memories of the violent destruction of his family in China, the Chinaman is able to disarm the threat Zuela poses to his life by barraging her with questions that reveal the economic consequences for her and her children were she to pursue a course that would ultimately kill him.

> "And after I gone, what you do? Who take care of you? . . . Who feed you? Put shelter over you? . . . Who take care of your children? . . . Who feed your children? . . . Who put roof over their head? . . . Who put shoes on their feet? . . . Who give you money to send them to school? . . . I leave you nothing when I dead. You walk the street like a beggar." He saw her shoulders sag to her bosom. He saw her swallow her rage, bottle and cork it.
>
> "Your children sell payme on the corner of Charlotte Street to feed you. The girls end up like you. . . . Worse than you. . . . Your mother dead. Who you go back to? Who take care of you? . . . I do it when I want to. . . . I have you when I want you."[18]

The unbalanced exchange of economic power that is implicit in the depiction of the Chinese shopkeeper's relationship to the village women is hardly new. Colonial discourses had earlier suggested that Chinese businesspeople would drive the "native West Indians" out of business, thereby establishing an early boundary between "native" and "Chinese" West Indians on the basis of financial interests.[19] Although the fact that the Chinese communities throughout the West Indies overall became closely associated with the small retail ("shop") sector of West Indian economies, the perception of an economic division of interests between the Chinese and other West Indians would prove to be particularly strong in Jamaica where the dominance of "the Chinese shop" in the early twentieth century has been well-documented. In fact, antipathy to the Chinese shopkeeper in Jamaica would reveal itself in two widespread riots in the twentieth century in Jamaica, events that do not have a parallel in Guyana or Trinidad.[20] As such, it is unsurprising that the depiction of the Chinese as outsiders preying on native West Indian self-sufficiency, advancement, and interests is one of the most common images in West Indian literature, regardless of the region from which such literary texts emerge.

The image of the Chinese as financial predators is key to understanding the tension in Earl McKenzie's short story "Platform Shoes" in which Donovan's hopes to improve his economic situation are symbolized by his desire for literal elevation—the platform shoes he wants to buy. His boss, Mr. Chin, directly prevents him from achieving this goal by beating him in the card game, thereby ensuring that Donovan does not have the money to buy the shoes. The loss of his paycheck at the hands of Mr. Chin sends Donovan on a downward spiral that culminates in Mr. Chin shooting him as an intruder. The shooting leaves Donovan permanently lame and therefore unemployable and dashes all hope for financial betterment with which the story began.

That Mr. Chin brings down Donovan's chances for advancement on both a physical and a symbolic level is fairly obvious; however, it is clear that the reader is to see the conflict that is happening between the two men on a broader scale as well. In fact, the story begins with the image of Chinese invaders who have conquered the community financially when Donovan notes that the majority of the businesses on the street are either owned by Chinese businesspeople or housed in buildings owned by Chinese individuals. Similarly, although the term "Chinese" is used quite generally to describe anyone with phenotypical traits associated with the Far East in the Caribbean, one might also consider the workers' insistence on calling their abusive Korean employers "Chinese" regardless of their awareness of their true ethnic background in Alecia McKenzie's "Cho', Delsha, Man," as evidence of the deep roots of the image of Chinese economic exploitation in the West Indies.[21] It is this repetitive and ritualized depiction of the Chinese as financial exploiters found in fiction like "Platform Shoes" that creates a clear and powerful division between those identified as "real" West Indians and the outsiders who oppress them. Indeed, in many ways, the Chinese are represented as a force that must be overcome in the process of coming-into-being as a nation.

The implicit positioning of the Chinese shopkeeper as an outsider to the nation's concerns and experiences also grounds V. S. Naipaul's critique of West Indian revolutionary spirit in the novel *Guerrillas*. The novel's revolution is supposedly based on an opposition between the "haves" and the "have-nots." These positions also designate who it is that "belongs" in the "revolutionary nation," namely the have-nots. To fit himself into this nation space, Jimmy, the son of a Chinese shopkeeper and the leader of the so-called revolution, must demonstrate that he is one of the have-nots. He attempts to do so on the basis of his shopkeeper background when he claims, "I'm a worker. I was born in the backroom of a Chinese grocery."[22] It is this shop background that Jimmy claims inspired him to work for revolutionary change on his island. The reactions of other characters on the island, particularly Meredith, make it clear, however, that Jimmy's shopkeeper background indicates the revolution's emptiness, as the traditional position of the shopkeeper in the West Indies is understood to be one of the "haves," not one of the "have-nots."

At one point, Jimmy tells Jane that because his father was a shopkeeper, "I suppose that's why I've always felt hungry."[23] Jane, a representative of the uncommitted foreign liberal, accepts the romantic image he creates largely because she has no true interest in the revolution other than as a fad of the moment. If she had, she would have realized that, as the child of a shopkeeper, Jimmy would have been one of the least "hungry" people on the island. By contrast, Meredith is painfully aware of this reality. His words demonstrate the huge gap between Jimmy and the

Black masses that renders Jimmy's position as a Black revolutionary ridiculous.

> I used to envy Jimmy. And most boys were like me, eh. A shop—how could a thing like that ever go bust? A shop had everything. It was a place where your mother sometimes sent you to get things on trust. . . . Jimmy's mother was a very pretty woman. . . . I used to envy old Leung, and I used to think: You can get a woman like that only if you have money, if you have a shop. To me that was just a fact of life, that our women went to live with Chinese shopkeepers. There was nothing you could do about it. Nobody had to tell me anything. I knew that side of life was closed to me.[24]

In this passage, Meredith establishes the distance between the Chinese community and the Black masses along a boundary between "us" and "them, "our side" and "their side," that articulates a division of financial interests and experiences; and in so doing, he bars the Chinese from being members of the nation.

Jimmy's Chinese shopkeeper background is also significant to Naipaul's assertion of the futility of West Indian revolution on a more basic level. Simply put, Jimmy does not have the necessary knowledge to lead a revolution that is supposedly based on the land. This suggests that a true dismantling of West Indian societies' oppressive regimes, their legacy of the colonial experience, would require a total change of lifestyle and ambitions represented as a return to the land and communal living. The choice of a Chinese shopkeeper to lead such a movement points to the insincerity that lies at the movement's heart because, as a shopkeeper, Jimmy appears to have no real understanding of such a lifestyle. Overall, in *Guerrillas*, Chineseness is so integrally connected to shopkeeping that "being Chinese" becomes a trope that points to the foreseeable failure of the communal revolution and, by extension, the hypocrisy of the revolution.

The association between the shopkeeper and exploitative

power is made more explicit in Patricia Powell's *The Pagoda*, where Lowe's position as shopkeeper converges with his intimate relationships with the two symbols of colonial power in the novel, Miss Sylvie and Cecil. The dramatic burning of Lowe's shop that opens the novel reveals both the villagers' belief that Lowe holds an oppressive position over them and their resistance to "how the Chinaman take advantage of we."[25] Indeed, the burning of the shop suggests the villagers' main agenda: namely, their desire to ensure that the Chinese community, represented by Lowe, is unable to step into a position of power over them at a time when European control seems to be waning in the colony. This agenda is made even more explicit in the fears that Lowe's son-in-law expresses when he learns of Lowe's plans to build a Chinese meetinghouse: "At first is farming and such. Then next thing shop, and before you know, a little shop in every blasted corner you turn. Now is school and property. Soon you have my people working for you on the estates, cleaning for you in the big house. Calling you massa and such."[26]

Lowe also realizes that the villagers' fears and ambitions affect whether or not he is accepted as belonging in the community when he considers how his moving in with Miss Sylvie will look to his neighbors.

> [T]he people would never trust him now. Here he was Chinese, and here he was cohabiting with this white-skinned woman, Miss Sylvie, and here he was now living in the biggest house in the district with a dark-skinned maid and dark-skinned yard boy. How to explain to the villagers when the very way he and Miss Sylvie lived up there in that house bore stark resemblance to a history and a way of life he did not live through but had heard as a story unfolding so many times at the shop he felt close to it. How to show them that he hadn't changed, wasn't changing, was still the Lowe they knew, he wasn't emulating the behavior of the ruling class even if it seemed that way, it was only that he wanted something better for [his daughter].[27]

Regardless of what Lowe's true intentions might be, the Blacks around him read his behavior as threatening to their own ambitions. In fact, it very much suits them to portray Lowe as an oppressive force in their community, because it gives them a focal point at which to vent their frustrations and anger when times get difficult.

In conjunction with this image of the Chinese as an overt economic threat is the more subtle idea that the Chinese are economic parasites fattening their bank accounts off the misery of other West Indians. It is an image that both reinforces the idea that the Chinese are ultimately a financial threat to the well-being of average West Indians and that the Chinese are not "real" West Indians. To that end, an oft-repeated complaint in West Indian literature is that the Chinese send their money to China instead of reinvesting it within the West Indian communities in which they make their money. The words of Miss Ethelrida in Alfred Mendes' *Black Fauns* sum up this common representation of the Chinese; she reminds the other women of the barrack-yard: "[Y]ou know how them Chinee is, how they does keep their money in de house instead of putting it in de bank; how dey does go back to China wit' all de money when they make it an don't spend a damn cent here; how they employee only Chinee like themselves in their shop, all you know dat."[28] Ultimately, both the general image of the Chinese as an economic enemy and the specific image of the Chinese as an economic parasite represent West Indian nationhood in terms of a story of financial oppression. Financial struggle is depicted as the definitive West Indian experience. By portraying the Chinese as being distanced from this struggle—indeed, as often being the cause of this struggle—such depictions reinforce a boundary between the Chinese and the "real" West Indians.

Often, it is the little details of a text that are used to suggest a vast distance in economic experiences between the Chinese and other West Indians, such as those found in the comparison between Laura and the unseen Chinese woman, Mary, in *Miguel Street*. Both women are the mothers of eight children, but whereas Laura cares for her brood with a rough tenderness born out of her struggle for financial security, Mary is portrayed as having the financial stability to lavish more care on her children: "Mary took really good care of her children and never spoke harshly to them. But Mary, mark you, had a husband who owned a shop, and Mary could afford to be polite and nice to her children after stuffing them full of chop-suey and chow-min, and chow-fan, and things with names like that."[29]

A similar distinction occurs in Ismith Khan's "The Magic Ring," where the large chasm of financial experience between the boy's father and the shopkeeper accounts for their vastly different treatments of the boy. This depiction of a somewhat generous Chinese shopkeeper finds a parallel in Chin-Quee, the grocer in *The Hills of Hebron*, who although generally depicted as cruel and quarrelsome, has enough money to lavish a certain amount of physical care on his daughter. Even more explicit is the short story "Song of Sixpence," by Samuel Selvon. In this story, calypso is identified as the expression of true Trinidadian experience and identity, and the lyrics of the story's calypso make it clear that the defining experience of the "real" or "true" Trinidadian is that of financial difficulty: "It had a time in this colony/ When everybody have money excepting me/ I can't get a work no matter how I try/ It look as if good times pass me by."[30]

"Good times," however, are never presented as "passing by" the members of the Chinese community in this story. When Razor Blade is rich, for example, he spends his money at high-class Chinese restaurants; when times are bad, he looks for food in the cheaper Chinese restaurants. Whether or not times are good or bad for the other members of the community, the Chinese appear to keep making money. Even when Razor Blade flees the restaurant without paying for his meal, it is made clear that it is the waitress who will end up bearing the cost of the meal out of her wages, not the Chinese owner.

In a similar fashion, the relationship between Black village women and the Chinese men they encounter is often presented in a manner that suggests that the Chinese communities' financial experience is entirely different from that of other West Indians. In Mendes' "Her Chinaman's Way," for example, Maria's involvement with Wing is based on her belief that because of their liaison, her financial situation will improve enough for her to move out of the barrack-yard. Physical distance parallels financial distance in Eric Walrond's "The Wharf Rats." Maura's fantasies of escaping the boxcar tenements of the West Indian labor camp focus on San Tie because she believes that by marrying him, she will literally cross over to the "right side of the track."[31] In "Stuck in the Maid's Room," by Alecia McKenzie, physical space is again used to mark out the distance of financial experience. The average West Indian remains trapped in a space of servitude while the Chinese have an entirely different experience of mobility, most obviously demonstrated when their money allows them to flee the country when times get tough.[32]

"I Ain' Dat Sort": Maintaining a Social Distance

The financial distance between the Chinese and other West Indians that positions the Chinese as alien to a "true" West Indian experience is also repeated in depictions of sociocultural distance. On occasion, this distancing of the Chinese is created by representing them as being particularly exotic and mysterious. In "The Beauty Contest," by Shiva Naipaul, for example, the contestant from Ma Fong Restaurant stands out from the other competitors because of the Chinese elements in her costume, while in Khan's "The Magic Ring" and Paule Marshall's "British Guiana," the presence of the Chinese is associated with such inexplicable and supernatural elements as the raised Chinese calligraphy on the ring and Sybil and Ling's eerie ability to foresee Motley's imminent death. Such exoticization, however, remains somewhat rare. More commonly, the Chinese are depicted as being outsiders to the sociocultural norms and values of other West Indians.

One of the more obvious examples of such representation is that of Hong Wing in Mendes' "Her Chinaman's Way." The suggestion that Hong Wing is depraved, deviant, and somewhat diabolical because he holds to an entirely different moral standard from the other members of the community is established early in the text. For example, throughout their relationship, Maria is depicted as being constantly afraid of Wing, aware of a dangerous undercurrent that pulses through his being. Maria's fear of Wing is a significant indication that she is in the presence of something unnaturally sinister because it is made clear throughout the story that Maria has never been afraid of any of her previous lovers, including those who had physically abused her. It is, however, Wing's abnormal hatred toward his own child, culminating in his murdering the baby out of spite, which establishes the idea that Wing operates outside of commonly recognized standards of morality and decency held by the other West Indians around him.

As the story unfolds, Wing makes the strange complaint that Maria loves their baby more than she loves him, and, on at least one occasion, Maria suspects Wing of deliberately hurting their child. In general, however, Maria disregards Wing's complaints because the idea that a father could possibly be murderously jealous of his child's relationship with its mother is beyond her moral frame of reference. In contrast to the depiction of Wing's perverted love, Mendes takes particular care to establish the fact that Maria subscribes to many of the conventional norms of West Indian society, even though, as barrack-yard women, she and her friends are outside the boundaries of respectable middle-class society. Thus, Maria is said to go to mass regularly and is depicted as having a strong, protective instinct for her child. More important, when Philogen and Maria plot how Maria might escape from Wing and Maria mistakenly believes that Philogen is suggesting that they murder him, Philogen responds quickly: "I ain' dat sort; I respec' human life, if even it's only a Chink."[33] Thus, a contrast between Wing, as a representative of Chinese morality, and Philogen and Maria, as representatives of West Indian conventional morality, is established along this vastly different attitude toward the sanctity of human life.

It is important to understand that Wing's attitude and behavior is not just a quirk of his individual character but is to be understood as being somehow connected to his status as a Chinese man. Mendes' representations of Hong Wing suggest such a reading on a number of occasions throughout the story. Even the choice of the title—"Her Chinaman's Way," rather than something more individually specific like "Hong Wing's Way"—suggests that Wing's character and behavior are somehow indicative of any "Chinaman." Similarly, the adjectives used to describe Wing, words like "sleek," "mysterious," and "enigmatic" are not accidental. Rather, they draw on language that is closely associated with Orientalist productions of Asianness. Indeed, just as Orientalist discourse relies on images of "the Oriental" as threatening the moral fabric of the West, Wing, as a generic representative of the members of the Chinese shopkeeping class in Trinidad, is not only outside of conventional West Indian norms, he also represents a direct danger to such mores and values.

Another means by which Mendes suggests that the Chinese are an unassimilable foreign element in Trinidad is the depiction of Maria's inability to ever truly know or understand Wing. Specifically, part of Maria's inability to be at ease with Wing lies in the fact that she cannot comprehend him. Mendes writes: "She had felt that she would never get to understand him. . . . [T]hough she had been living with him for such a long time, she had never been able to understand him."[34] Contrasting this fundamental divide between Maria and Wing is the relationship that Maria has with Adolphus, the Creole man with whom she embarks on an affair. Of Adolphus, it is simply said that Maria "understood him well."[35] Maria and Adolphus' ability to understand each other is grounded in their shared culture. This is made evident in Maria's daydream of how the two might spend Christmas day together—eating pelau and drinking rum—activities in which it appears she would not engage with Wing.

That Maria's relationship with the two men is differentiated by the presence or absence of a shared culture is also evidenced by the fact that Maria and Adolphus share an understanding of appropriate behavior between women and men that is lacking in Maria's relationship with Wing. Maria retains a certain amount of control in her relationships with other Trinidadian men that is entirely missing in her relationship with Wing. With these men, there is an understanding that women need not be entirely submissive to their male partners. For example, upon learning that her previous lover was keeping another woman, Maria gives him such a thorough "cussing" that he is described as slinking "off like a whipped puppy."[36] Even Adolphus is portrayed as exhibiting a certain level of docility before Maria. Such gestures are not, however, present in Maria's interaction with Wing. Indeed, the lack of common cultural reference points leaves Maria and Wing largely unknowable to each other—a reality that reinforces the depiction of Wing as an alien presence in the cultural landscape.

Interestingly, the social distance that defines the Chinese as a type of social outcast in the West Indies is sometimes reaffirmed by portraying the Chinese as having a certain degree of social flexibility that is unavailable to those members of the community who are firmly entrenched in its social hierarchies. It is a flexibility that appears to be based on the idea that the Chinese have no real place in the social hierarchy left by the colonial order. One of the most striking depictions in this regard is that of Olga Yen Tip in Edgar Mittelholzer's *A Morning in the Office.* Olga is apparently permitted certain social freedoms that would be clearly problematic if they were indulged in by other characters in the text. For example, she speaks to Miss Henery and Mrs. Hinckson with a familiarity that would never be tolerated from Mr. Jagabir, much less the office boy or the office cleaner. Olga also seems to move, to some extent, within Miss Henery's and Mrs. Hinckson's social circles even though Olga is not a member of the respectable colored middle class that the two women represent. Olga even freely gossips with Miss Henery about attending a social function at which a man who wants to marry Miss Henery was present. Equally significant in this regard is the comment that Olga "had her own friends—Chinese as well as colored middle-class—and there were at least three young men, extremely eligible husbands, very much bent on marrying her."[37] What is interesting about this comment is that Mittelholzer never makes it clear whether these potential spouses are Chinese or colored, seeming to suggest that such a detail is irrelevant in Olga's situation. This is a significant breach from the rigid social boundaries that must be maintained by all the other characters in the text, particularly in light of the fact that it is made clear that Miss Bisnauth is expected to marry an Indo-Trinidadian, and Miss Henery and Mrs. Hinckson, the widow, are expected to marry colored, upper middle-class gentlemen.[38]

The image of the Chinese as living parallel but somewhat separate lives from other West Indians that is suggested in the depiction of Olga is performed more explicitly in a number of other texts. A telling example of this distance occurs in *Guerrillas*, for example, when, while in England, Jimmy describes a childhood game in which the complexion of one's future spouse was said to be indicated by a banana peel. Jimmy tells the story as part of his anticolonial revolutionary rhetoric, using it as evidence of the absorption of colonial values with regard to color and complexion in the West Indies; however, the story also highlights how very different Jimmy's life experiences have been from the Black masses he supposedly represents when Meredith claims that neither he nor his fellow Black Creoles have ever heard of the game, much less played it. Meredith's total ignorance of such a game reemphasizes the idea that a significant distance exists between the Chinese community's experience in the West Indies and that of the everyday Black Creole—a difference so extreme that Meredith claims that "when Jimmy talked about this country, I couldn't recognize it."[39] *A Morning in the Office* suggests a similar distance in social experiences for Olga's wealthy relatives. Clearly, the Grangers live a lifestyle similar to that of other West Indians of their financial standing; however, it is unclear as to whether or not their lives are actually integrated with other West Indians around them. In *Crown Jewel*, by Ralph de Boissière, however, no such vagueness exists. William Hoo is depicted as being wealthy enough to own estates, race horses, and a home in the exclusive St. Clair neighborhood, but the novel makes it clear that despite his possessions, he is rejected by his wealthy West Indian neighbors.

Chineseness as Politically Incorrect

Crown Jewel's performance of Chineseness is particularly important for this study because the novel fictionalizes a nascent Trinidadian independence movement and national identity. Both are portrayed as developing directly out of working-class consciousness and the labor unrest of the 1930s. Despite the seeming inclusiveness of this site of nationhood—as evidenced by the individuals of various class and ethnic groups involved in the struggle—the Chinese in this novel are consistently situated in opposition to, or outside of, working-class political and labor interests. In the end, it is *Crown Jewel*'s depiction of the Chinese community as being outside of (and antagonistic toward) the labor and political concerns of the other West Indians in the novels that is used to identify the political community being defined as "the nation" and to situate their narrative of belonging within a struggle against labor exploitation.

All the Chinese characters who appear in *Crown Jewel* are represented as exploiting members of the working class, and, as such, they become symbols of the power that the exploited laborers are struggling against to come into existence as a nation. For example, Hoo takes advantage of Elena's desperate need for employment by paying her significantly less than the previous employee in the post and by giving her measly bonuses. On a more subtle level, Hoo's year-end party provides particularly dramatic evidence of the tyrannical power that he exercises over his workers. The party, supposedly thrown to thank his employees for their hard work throughout the year, becomes little more than a demonstration of their vulnerability to Hoo. Hoo expects the workers to make excessively flattering toasts in his honor, and it is clear that one's job depends on satisfying Hoo's whims in this regard. Indeed, when Elena fails to make a satisfactory speech, she is promptly fired. One of the more poignant moments in this scene occurs when the workers enact the only act of resistance they seem capable of—namely, making the weak joke that Hoo is serving horsemeat at his banquet. What makes this moment particularly important in terms of representing the Chinese as the exploiters and oppressors of those being defined as the nation is the reader's awareness of the workers' defenselessness despite their laughter; for the reader is very conscious of the fact that even if Hoo were serving them horsemeat, the employees would be too afraid of losing their jobs to refuse to eat it.

A similar separation from working-class interests is evident in the behavior of Chin Toon during the strike. Chin Toon so disdains the workers that he initially does not bother to attend the labor negotiations. When he does deign to attend, both he and the other Chinese baker quickly demonstrate that they are totally uninterested in the concerns of the workers; or, as the other baker puts it explicitly: "What do Chin Toon and I care about all of you and your resolutions?"[40] Chin Toon's total alienation from working-class concerns is most obviously illustrated when he simply closes his bakery rather than raise wages, claiming confidently that, "When their bellies get empty they will come to me—cheap, cheap."[41]

As if to ensure that the reader absolutely understands that the Chinese are not members of the nation, it is not only Chin Toon, the other Chinese baker, and Hoo who are depicted as being political outsiders. Even Yankee, the Chinese friend of the novel's labor leader Le Maître, is distanced from those who are being identified with the nation. He does not provide his hall free of charge for the meetings that Le Maître holds, for example. Similarly, he takes advantage of Popi's desperate straits when he hires Popi as a smuggler who takes all the risk for Yankee's illegal business activities. Dramatically, in the scene when the mob bursts into Yankee's shop looking for kerosene with which they will burn the abusive policeman, Yankee's only reaction is to hide his money in the rice and to guard it with a knife, an action that illustrates how far removed he is from the passions of the crowd.[42]

Other details of Chinese distance from working-class interests scattered throughout the novel contribute to an overall performance of Chinese alienation from national interests. For example, no Chinese character appears before the royal commission investigating labor conditions in the West Indies, although an Indian character is present along with some Blacks. Similarly, the novel portrays only Indian shopkeepers feeding the protesters on their long march to Government House—a point that is even more significant if one realizes that all the previous references to shopkeepers in the novel had been about Chinese characters. In another more poignant scene, Elena is described as packing up her and her mother's threadbare possessions in the night as they plan to flee their residence for cheaper accommodations. Across the street, well-dressed Chinese women alight from cars to attend a dance, totally oblivious to the cares that mark Elena's life. Together, the representations of Chinese characters in *Crown Jewel* depict not only individuals who are at odds with the nation, but an entire community that stands apart from the nation.

The perceived distance of the Chinese community from the political community that is deemed the nation in *Crown Jewel* is, as suggested above, also central to understanding Naipaul's novel *Guerrillas*. Set on a fictional West Indian island, the novel depicts a landscape in which any real revolutionary progress toward a revitalized and revamped society has become arrested; it has been replaced, instead, by a national and international game of make-believe revolution. Thus, the former colony is locked in an obscene cycle of violence with England, its former colonial ruler. Although both take turns at playing violator and violated, ultimately such play does not overthrow the original imbalance of power in their relationship. To establish his idea that there is a fundamental emptiness at the heart of West Indian "revolutions," Naipaul peoples his novel with absurd characters: a guerrilla activist who respects authority and is more interested in making gestures of revolution than in actually effecting revolutionary results; an English liberal with no political views who treats her politics as a fashion trend; rioters who restrain themselves from causing any real damage and wait for some authority figure to descend on them and "dish out licks and pick up the pieces"; and a Chinese leader of a so-called Black revolution, Jimmy Ahmed.[43]

Most critics recognize Jimmy as a figure of "inauthenticity and pretensions"; however, they do not read Jimmy's Chineseness as being one of the means by which Naipaul points out the falseness of the revolution that Jimmy purportedly leads.[44] As discussed earlier, Naipaul portrays Jimmy in such a manner that one cannot help but conclude that there is something fundamentally erroneous in the idea of a Chinese shopkeeper "in tune with the aspirations of black people."[45] Jimmy himself also seems to realize the falseness of his position—that his identity is "a matter of smoke and mirrors"—when he writes in the persona of "Clarissa" following his first encounters with Jane.[46] Jimmy portrays himself as distanced and superior to the mass of Black revolutionaries that he supposedly leads by imagining Jane's (that is, "Clarissa's") reaction to him in the following language: "I am amazed at . . . the way he gets these black louts to respect him and behave with discipline. . . . You wouldn't believe that he can be so *different from them*" (emphasis added); and, on another occasion, "[H]e is like a prince helping these poor and indigent black people, they're so shiftless, no one will help them *least of all their own*" (emphasis added).[47] The key point of these passages is their depiction of Jimmy as being separate and distinct from these "black louts"; they are not his "own," and by extension, neither is their revolution. Indeed, the novel specifies that while living on the island as a young man, Jimmy had not particularly associated with the Black masses but had tried to connect to the Chinese community and their issues, "talking about going to China to advise Mao Tse-tung," a detail that reveals how very distanced Jimmy really is from the concerns and interests of the Black people he supposedly leads.[48] Indeed, Jimmy only becomes a "Black Revolutionary" when the identity is created for him while living in England. Nevertheless, despite his failed attempts to be either a Chinese Revolutionary or a Black Revolutionary, Jimmy cannot truly be said to be "without personality . . . only a haphazard succession of roles."[49] Instead, his Chineseness is represented as an absolute and unchangeable characteristic that ultimately renders it so impossible for him to be a Black revolutionary that he must be dismissed during the riots as "just another Chinaman."[50]

Importantly, Jimmy's Chinese background also positions him outside of the historical frame of reference in which the political nation is being located. For example, the posters featuring Jimmy are captioned with the words: "I'm nobody's slave or stallion."[51] The words supposedly encapsulate the revolution's official spirit of defiance and a challenge to the history of slavery, its dehumanization of the Black man, and the legacy of financial, political, and social struggle for Blacks that it left behind. Under the picture of a Chinese man, however, despite the fact that he is made to appear "more Negroid than he was," they take on an empty ring.[52] Thus, the distance of Jimmy from the very history that he claims as justification for the revolution becomes just another means of drawing attention to the absurdity of the revolution and Jimmy's place within it.

Just as the acceptance of Jimmy as the leader of a Black revolution by English liberals exposes their lack of commitment to revolutionary ideals, the attitudes toward the Chinese on the part of the Blacks is used to indicate their lack of real desire for revolutionary change as well as the perception that the Chinese are excluded from the nation. For example, Harry suggests that the rioters will focus their rage on the Chinese as immediate representatives of the system that exploits them, but he predicts that the Chinese are not really in danger from the rioters. Although a couple of Chinese shops might be burned down, Harry does not believe that there will be any actual loss of life. In fact, after the so-called riot, Roche's awareness that "the city showed little damage . . . even in the streets of the Chinese wholesale food shops . . . though a shop had been blackened at the pavement level, its upper floors still looked whole" becomes a vivid means of revealing the rioters' lack of commitment to tearing down the systems that oppress them at the same time that it positions the Chinese as outsiders to the political nation.[53]

The Chinese as the Face of Alienation

The distance from other West Indians that is attributed to the Chinese in literary texts also manifests itself in the depiction of the Chinese as being a fundamentally alien presence in the West Indies. Indeed, Chinese characters are sometimes depicted as the only individuals who can see the larger themes and issues within West Indian experiences because of their purported distance from them. Such is the case in the novels *Pan Beat*, *Mr. On Loong*, and *The Pagoda*.

Pan Beat, by Marion Patrick Jones, tells a story of West Indian disillusionment caused by the empty ambitions and dreams of the first postindependence generation through the reunion of a group of former sixth form friends. Their reacquaintance forces them to acknowledge the "mask of living" behind which they have hidden their shallow, insecure, and meaningless lives.[54] One of the members of their group is, however, missing from this reunion. It is Dave Chow, who had, years before, realized the emptiness of their ambitions when he concluded that: "One is always whoring for something . . . when we grow up we will sell ourselves for some damn thing."[55] Rather than end up like that, Chow chooses to commit suicide early in life.

Chow's ability to see so clearly and so early the falseness of his and his friends' ambitions is linked to the fact that he is fundamentally an outsider among them. True, he is a member of their sixth form steel band and even dates one of the Black girls in the group, but an aura of alienation continues to surround him. Chow does not really fit in. The middle-class parents, for example, blame Chow for the existence of the disreputable and socially questionable steel band, "instinctively, because that Chinese man couldn't be trusted," while Chow is specifically remembered as having been "a slight Chinese boy *always out of everything.* His pan needed tuning, he never played football, he never joined the cadets" (emphasis added).[56] The repetitive attention given to designating Chow as "Chinese" in both examples is used to emphasize the idea that Chow's alienation in the community is linked directly to his ethnic background.

Robert Standish is much more obvious in connecting a state of alienation with the condition of "being Chinese" in the West Indies in *Mr. On Loong.* John lives a solitary life on the fictional Newcastle Island, existing in a state of neutrality between the Black and White elements of the population specifically because he is the one Chinese man on the island. Although it may be an exaggeration to claim, as one reviewer does, that John is "too much like Confucius" to care about his solitary state of existence, on one of the rare occasions that John does complain about being different, his friend confirms that John's Chinese status is at the root of his alienation and isolation.[57] "Being Chinese," according to his friend, allows John to live a life without labels; that is, to live a life that is distanced from the conventions and limitations of West Indian society.

> In this world, for reasons I don't profess to understand, people love labels. They like to identify their fellow creatures by labels. They like to say: here is a black man, a white man, or a yellow man. They like to call their fellows heathen or Christians; Catholics or Protestants; Jews or Gentiles. They insist upon wearing a political label. They group occupations according to whether they are respectable, or outside the pale. . . . Now you complain of being made to feel "different" and I tell you . . . you are different.[58]

As with Dave Chow, John's distance from the divisive passions that characterize the West Indian community of the novel is linked to his Chinese blood. Standish makes John's neutrality a racialized trait in the following manner: The Chinese "are not so definitive as the rest of the world. They do not insist that black is black and white is white and that there are no intermediate shades. The greys exist in Chinese thought in an infinite number."[59] Indeed, for the entire novel, John lives his life in a "grey zone," permanently distanced from the rest of the population, "a perfect neutral."[60] Like Olga Yen Tip, this distance is revealed in a certain freedom that John has to move outside of the racialized social circles that constrain life on Newcastle Island. Thus, John freely gives money to the charities he is interested in, regardless of whether or not they help the Black or White segments of the population, and hires and fires employees based on ability rather than skin color. However, John's ability to live "without labels" that his Chinese status permits also leaves him essentially alienated with no real social circle on the island.

In *The Pagoda*, by Patricia Powell, the idea that the Chinese communities are aliens in the West Indies also plays an important role in contextualizing the concerns raised in the novel. Essentially, Powell explores the construction of gendered identities in her tale of Lowe's life. From the beginning of his life, gender and sexual boundaries for Lowe have always been somewhat porous and mutable such that for most of his life, although he was born a female, Lowe has lived as a man. Personally, I find it interesting that Powell would use a Chinese character for such an exploration of gendered identities in the West Indies. I cannot help but ask myself, what made it more attractive or more workable for her to use a person of Chinese ethnicity to conduct her inquiry? Why not use a member of the more numerous ethnic groups that populate the island?

It might not be possible to answer such questions absolutely; nevertheless, I do wonder if Powell was not tapping into the long tradition of representing the Chinese as outsiders and aliens in the West to explore the questions that she wants to raise. In other words, Powell might have chosen to use a Chinese character because, if the Chinese are understood to be symbols of alienation, it would reinforce Lowe's sense of estrangement and isolation as a transgendered individual in that community. Lowe's outsider status in the community as a Chinese man parallels and reinforces his outsider status to conventional gender and sexual norms. Similarly, as outsiders to the greater West Indian communities, the Chinese are often represented as being largely unknowable. This mystery heightens Powell's exploration of gender and sexual identities because it draws attention to the question of whether or not such identities ever actually reveal anything meaningful about the individuals who wear them or whether, despite the labels we wear, we all remain essentially unknowable. Finally, members of the Chinese communities in the West Indies often have a shopkeeper identity imposed upon them, much like the name "Mr. Chin," just because they are Chinese in the West Indies. The imposition of this identity parallels the imposition of the different sexual and gender identities that Lowe struggles with and brings attention to the questions of how and who gets to construct identities—questions that are central to this novel. If Powell is using Lowe's Chinese ethnicity, complete with its purported alienation, as a symbolic device to further develop the gender and sexual identity issues that she wants to explore, then, in this regard, "being Chinese" is not simply just an ethnic fact; rather, for Lowe, as with other Chinese characters, alienation and nonbelonging become an inherent aspect of Chineseness in the West Indies.

As part of the process of asserting the place of their respective nations in the global political arena, West Indian nationalists were highly aware of the need to create narratives that would give meaning to the chaotic modern histories, shaped directly by colonialism, that were their sociopolitical legacy. One of the ways they did so was to link the experiences of slavery and indenture to independence, presenting their anticolonial position as a natural development in a long history of resistance to exploitation. Thus they could claim that the individuals who made up the nation were "the product of a very old and enduring colonial era."[61] The unequal economic conditions engendered by colonialism for West Indian populations, however, continued long after independence, and so the narrative of struggle for survival, especially in economic terms, continued (and continues) to have a particular resonance. Since the Chinese were so often involved in the small retail trade industry in the early twentieth century and seemed to literally oppose desires, ambitions, and hopes of the average working-class West Indian as they stood on the other side of the counter, it was easy to co-opt their representations into a performance of a narrative of belonging constructed around a struggle against exploitation. A 1936 newspaper article that appeared in Jamaica's *Daily Gleaner* made such a distinction between belonging and nonbelonging clear when it marked out the difference between native and nonnative in terms of economic concerns.

> [O]ur Chinese citizens have embarked upon trade and trade only. By doing so they have swept out of existence the native traders for the most part, and men capable of entering this line of business find themselves today with no opportunity of trading in their own country. . . . We admit at once that the Chinese born in this country has a very strong case to put forward if anyone contends that he has no place in Jamaica. He has a place. But he is expected to feel as a Jamaican and to view the country's future as something which intimately concerns himself and must intimately concern his children. (Quoted in Lynch-Campbell, 94)[62]

The representations of Chinese shopkeepers that appear in West Indian literature are part of this narrative performance. Encounter after literary encounter with alienated, leering, exploitative, calculating, aloof, dangerous Chinese shopkeepers becomes a ritualized gesture that gives substance to the ideas expressed in a narrative of national oppression. These literary scenes are an everyday or banalized means of setting national boundaries. As Billig might put it, the representations of the Chinese as national outsiders "flag the nation" in its intangible story of struggle, survival, and resistance.

And yet, a close examination of West Indian literature reveals that this performance of belonging is unstable. Fictional representations of Chinese participating in, sharing with, and building up the lives of other community members also exist, seemingly subverting and destabilizing the knowledge of their outsidership established so effectively in the Orientalized depiction of the Chinese shopkeeper. The ambivalence in the depiction of the relationship between the Chinese and other West Indians captured in this representational shift need not, however, be interpreted as disruptive; rather, we can read these alternative representations of Chineseness as a performance within an entirely different national narrative, one in which belonging is connected to intercultural exchange.

3 / "A Real Creolise Chinee": Establishing Creole Inclusiveness

. . . you is a real creolise Chinee.

—SAMUEL SELVON, *TURN AGAIN TIGER*

One of the paradoxes of imagining nationhood is that nations must be both similar and distinct from other nations.[1] In other words, to be recognized as a viable nation in the international arena, nations must somehow "look" like other nations and, at the same time, be recognizably distinct. Usually, this distinctiveness is claimed on the basis of a unique cultural identity—the national identity. Thus, it is not surprising that a recurring theme throughout West Indian literature is the validation and celebration of the region's cultural features, such as language use, food, and music, which are deemed to be the result of the particular contact and mixing of cultures that is the legacy of their colonial experience. For theorists, the cultural melding deemed to be at the heart of West Indian national identities is often identified as "creolization," and "being creole" is the end result of that process.[2]

In his discussion of cultural identity in the West Indies, Stuart Hall notes:

> We cannot speak for very long with any exactness about "one experience, one identity," without acknowledging its other side—the ruptures and discontinuities which consti-

> tute precisely, the Caribbean's "uniqueness." Cultural identity in this . . . sense, is a matter of "becoming" as well as of "being" . . . [existing in] the unstable points of identification or suture, which are made, within the discourse of history and culture. Not an essence but a positioning.[3]

Hall further argues that these "points of identification" or "positions" gain meaning because they exist in dialogue with one of three "présences" that relate to the region's colonial past: the "Présence Africaine"; the "Présence Européen"; and an ambiguous "Présence Américaine" or "New World" presence. This latter presence is defined as "the juncture-point where the many cultural tributaries meet . . . the space where the creolizations and assimilations and syncretisms were negotiated."[4] It is at this coming together of cultural tributaries that Hall locates West Indian identity when he claims that the West Indies produces "a conception of 'identity' which lives with and through, not despite, difference. . . . One can only think here of what is uniquely—'essentially'—Caribbean: precisely the mixes of color, pigmentation, physiognomic type; the 'blends' of tastes that is Caribbean cuisine; the aesthetics of the 'cross-overs,' of 'cut-and-mix.'"[5]

Hall's idea of cultural "blending" as indicative of "West Indianness" is, of course, neither new nor limited to the field of Black British cultural studies. Indeed, Kamau Brathwaite's 1971 *The Development of Creole Society in Jamaica, 1770–1820* is generally considered to be the foundational statement on West Indian creole cultures. In this work, Brathwaite challenges the then conventional thinking that argued that the plantation system had created a segmented Jamaican society.[6] Instead, although he recognized power imbalances between the various groups in society, Brathwaite describes creolization as an organic synthesis of cultural elements, that is, "a cultural action . . . based upon the stimulus/response of individuals within the society to their environment and—as white/black, culturally discrete groups—to each other."[7] He concludes that by the eighteenth century, this process of exchange was already well established in Jamaica.

As part of his argument, Brathwaite recognizes the significance of creolization to Jamaica's national identity when he locates "the development of authentically local institutions" in Afro-Creole Jamaican culture and suggests that "[w]ith political power now in the hands of the black majority of the population [there was a possibility for] the development of a new parochial wholeness, a difficult but possible creole authenticity."[8] In other words, Brathwaite saw a creole culture as the defining feature of Jamaican identity. A similar tendency to locate West Indian national identities within a creole paradigm has been made from the earliest organized articulations of nationhood in the labor movements of the early twentieth century to popular tourist advertisements selling the Caribbean as a site of racial and ethnic harmony in contemporary times.

Although they might not have specifically used the term "creolization," nationalists regularly drew on the ideas behind the concept in creating narratives that sought to define their nation's identity. In his *History of the People of Trinidad and Tobago*, for example, Eric Williams identifies Trinidad as a unique meeting point of Carib, Arawak, and other Amerindian cultures and claims such cultural exchange to be the inheritance of the nation by making a link between that period and the more modern cultural interchanges among the Spanish, French, British, African, Chinese, Indian, and Portuguese who had come to inhabit the island by the time of independence. Similarly, in Jamaica, Norman Manley claimed that "[w]e have in Jamaica our own type of beauty, a wonderful mixture of African and European"; he then used this idea as the basis for his claim that "[t]he greatest contribution Jamaica and the West Indies can make to the world is to prove that a society can be made where black and white and brown and yellow live together as men and woman in mutual harmony and shared respect."[9] In Guyana, Forbes Burnham stated that it was out of the cultural diversity "of the peoples who comprise our country" that they would "create richer [cultural traditions], uniquely Guyanese."[10] In fact, the association between creolism and West Indian nationhood has become so accepted that it has been claimed, "Caribbean identity occurs within the discursive space of the 'Creole.'"[11]

Because of its emphasis on cross-cultural exchange, which presumes the existence of disparate ethnocultural groups, the creole narrative of nation appears, on the surface, to provide the perfect context for stylized social gestures that would represent the Chinese as belonging within West Indian nation spaces. However, it must also be recognized that the manner in which terms such as "creole" and "creolization" have been articulated in the West Indies is somewhat problematic. Specifically, creole identity has been largely understood as involving a mix of African and European cultural elements, thus marginalizing and/or excluding the contributions of the Chinese "to the mix." For example, despite Brathwaite's assertion that creolism allows "infinite possibilities . . . and many ways of asserting identity," he locates West Indian creole identities in a coming together of "white and black, master and slave."[12] Orlando Patterson's concept of segmentary and synthetic creolism also reifies the marginalization of other ethnic groups, including the Chinese, within the creole matrix when he divides West Indian culture into specifically Euro-Creole and Afro-Creole segments. He argues that synthetic creolization occurs from a coming together of elements from European institutional (such as educational, political, and legal structures) and Afro–West Indian expressive or symbolic (such as music, language, dance) cultural components. Thus, some theorists have been forced to conclude that for "the most part, the indigenous and diasporic communities with cultural and racial origins outside Africa and Europe remain, in representation and practice, outside Creole reality."[13] In other words, the banal performance of belonging subverts the inclusive national boundaries articulated in the creole national narrative.

This difficulty in constructing a narrative of nation that validates ethnic diversity, and, more specifically, the presence of the Chinese, is not unique to the West Indies. In the United States and Canada, for example, the struggle to accommodate Chineseness within national narratives has generally been expressed in debates concerning the possibilities and limitations of assimilation and multiculturalism. In the United States, the notion of a "Melting Pot" common national culture has long been recognized as requiring racialized ethnicities, like the Chinese, to assimilate to dominant Anglo-European-based cultural norms and values, that is, to be culturally invisible, although their physical features still render them "visible." The Model Minority myth that depicts the Chinese as easily achieving the "American Dream" has, for example, been criticized as one of the means of rendering the Chinese invisible by celebrating their perceived assimilation to mainstream American norms and values. In the late twentieth century, Americans became more interested in thinking through their national identity in terms of multiculturalism as an alternative to the melting pot. However, the experience of countries such as Canada, where multiculturalism is an official state policy, suggests that this narrative also offers only a "superficial national heterogeneity" for racialized ethnicities; further, its focus on recognizing separate and distinct cultures becomes a way "to other" traditionally marginalized ethnic groups while implicitly normalizing the values, practices, and perspectives of the dominant ethnocultural group.[14]

In Latin America, creolism as articulated in the West Indies finds its complement in the concept of *mestizaje* and *mestizo* nationalism, which, in a fashion similar to the creole narrative, celebrates "miscegenation or cultural mixture as the basis for conceiving a homogenous national identity out of a heterogenous population."[15] In Cuba, however, the place given to the Chinese within the articulation of *mestizo* national identity has also been problematic as *mestizaje* has been articulated in a way that prioritizes African and Creole contributions to the nation's cultural matrix. For example, despite the fact that there had been a visible Chinese presence fighting alongside other Cubans in the wars of independence and in the Cuban Revolution, recognition of a Chinese identity as different from a Cuban identity was perceived as threatening the development of Cuba's *mestizo* culture and was therefore actively suppressed. The "writing out" of Chineseness from the *mestizo* narrative was further complicated by the fact that prior to the Cuban Revolution, a large number of Chinese in Cuba had been involved in the small retail industry. In his study of the representation of the Chinese in Cuba's fictional landscapes, López-Calvo sums up these tensions when he writes, "Despite all of these contributions to national culture and independence, the degree of Creole and black acceptance and tolerance for the Chinese varied. . . . The Chinese subject was often met with ethnic hostility and mistrust . . . as he . . . was perceived by the national elites as an obstacle to their project of national homogeneity."[16]

Certainly, despite the existence of a creole narrative, the "writing out" of the Chinese from national spaces can be observed in West Indian literature. Nevertheless, the idea of nation in which a broad cultural melding constitutes the grounds on which belonging is performed continues to have a profound hold on West Indian imaginations. As we will see, this fact is attested to by the numerous fictional depictions of the Chinese as valid members of their communities. Indeed, such literary texts not only insist on the importance of the creole narrative for imagining national identities; they also embrace its more radical possibilities. Thus, the representations of the Chinese affirm the creole narrative by showing its potential to exist; celebrating its existence; or defining what norms, values, and behaviors are to be considered creole. In this latter case, Chinese characters often become the very measuring rod against which creolization can be affirmed, for behaviors, experiences, and cultural values gain credibility as being particularly "West Indian" when they are represented as affecting all members of the community, *even* the Chinese. It is this acting out symbolically of the "even"—this suggestion of reaching an outermost boundary of belonging when one reaches the Chinese—that makes images of Chinese participation in West Indian life a particularly potent means of confirming a creole national narrative in a banalized fashion.

"Cut-and-Mix": The Contact Spaces of Creolization

When Hall uses descriptions like "blends," "cross-overs," and "cut-and-mix" to describe the inherent hybridity of West Indian identities, he draws attention to the key concept behind creolization: the coming together of diverse ethnocultural components that then create something new.[17] As such, creolization can occur only in the contact spaces between ethnic groups. In West Indian literature, two sites associated with the Chinese are particularly significant in terms of establishing the potential for a creole culture to develop by facilitating this cultural contact: the shop and the school.

In *The Pagoda*, the deep hurt that Lowe experiences on the burning of his shop lies partially in his recognition that he had believed that the everyday exchanges in the shop were creating a new inclusive sense of community in which he would no longer be perceived as an outsider. For Lowe, however, the process of community building inherent in the creation of a creole culture is disrupted by his relationship with Cecil and Miss Sylvie. In Selvon's two novels, *A Brighter Sun* and its sequel *Turn Again Tiger*, however, the Chinese shopkeeper is not entangled in complicated relationships with figures of colonial power. Thus, in contrast to Lowe's situation where the slow process of creolization that was occurring in shop space is aborted, Selvon allows the development of creole culture in Tall Boy's shop to reach its logical conclusion, namely, Tall Boy's unqualified acceptance as belonging in the community.

Like *The Pagoda*, *A Brighter Sun* reveals the earliest stages in the development of a West Indian creole culture. One such indication of the existence of creolization occurs when Selvon notes that the Chinese shopkeeper has been given the nickname "Tall Boy." This is significant because Selvon also states that Chinese shopkeepers in Trinidad are usually known simply as "Chin." By giving him a personal nickname, the community has therefore already begun to claim him as their own. In *Turn Again Tiger*, this process of acceptance is completed when Tall

Boy is portrayed as engaged and participating in affairs that affect his community. For example, he shows a personal interest in Tiger—even interfering in a business deal when he feels that Tiger is going to get the short end of the deal, an action that would have been unimaginable in the first novel—and becomes involved in village political life. That this integration is caused by the everyday interactions that occur in the shop is revealed most explicitly in the events surrounding Tall Boy's decision to invite himself to Tiger's good-bye party.

The party will be the first that Tall Boy has attended since "nobody ever thought of asking Tall Boy [to any of the village parties]. Tall Boy was the symbol of the shop. . . . [T]hey never thought of him as a human being. . . . Nobody ever thought of asking Tall Boy to come and this hurt him though he kept it to himself."[18] Through these words, Selvon suggests that there is a tendency among the greater West Indian community to marginalize the Chinese presence in their midst, although he implies that this is done out of thoughtlessness rather than malice. This thoughtlessness, however, is also revealed to be an important part of the process of creolization; for, as the party scene demonstrates, it is the banality of the interactions that he has in the shop that eventually leads to the radical change of relationship between Tall Boy and the villagers.

Tall Boy arrives at the fete with some trepidation, "prepared for a lot of exclamation at his presence. But no one said anything. In fact, it was as if he had been attending every fete in the village."[19] There is no reaction to his appearance at the party because the villagers have, albeit unconsciously, already accepted him as one of their own. Tall Boy belongs. The everyday contact that Tall Boy has had with the villagers in the shop has, in a banal fashion, created a broader, creole understanding of community that can incorporate the once alien presence of Tall Boy. This change is affirmed, after the party when Joe, a Black Trinidadian tells Tall Boy, "[Y]ou is a real creolise Chinee," to which Tall Boy responds, "[Y]ou know that I just like one of you."[20] In fact, so successful has the shop been as a site of creolization that

Tall Boy and the villagers appear to be ready to move on to more cultural exchanges, for it is at this point that the two men make plans to visit each other's homes for dinner where they will share foods associated with their respective ethnic backgrounds: "peas and rice and callaloo" at Joe's, and "puck-chow and chowmin" at Tall Boy's.[21]

The important role that the Chinese shop plays in creolization is also central to Michael Anthony's short story "Many Things." Here, the dynamic process of cultural transaction that results in an inclusive sense of national belonging is represented in the relationship between shopkeeper Chin and the young village boy Allwyn. For most of the story, Chin is shown accommodating himself to his new West Indian environment. For example, Chin decorates the shop for Christmas, a celebration that was unknown to him in China. Anthony makes it clear that Chin's participation in the Christmas celebrations is not just for business purposes. Instead, Anthony portrays Chin as actually enjoying the holiday: "It had come to mean something to him too."[22] Similarly, Chin is portrayed testing out English words, greeting his wife with "Merry Christmas" and "Many things," the latter phrase apparently being the English translation of the traditional Chinese greeting on Name Day. However, since Anthony is celebrating the cultural transactions and transformations of creoleness, it is important that he also demonstrate the influence that Chin has on his new environment. This is accomplished through Chin's relationship with Allwyn and through the Chinese influences that are represented as making an impact on the Christmas celebrations.

The impact that Chin has on his community is most evident in the changing attitude of Allwyn toward him. By the end of the story, Chin is no longer an oddity or an object of scorn for Allwyn; he is deemed worthy of friendship and respect. Allwyn has made a place for Chin within his community. As Chin puts it, Allwyn "was getting used to him."[23] More important, Allwyn is also changed by Chin's presence. Midway through the story, Allwyn eavesdrops on Chin and his wife and overhears them exchanging the traditional Name Day greeting in Chinese. At first, Allwyn considers the foreign language to be an object of derision and determines to pull yet another prank on the shopkeeper. When the moment arrives, however, Allwyn changes his mind. Instead of treating Chin with derision, he bows in a traditional Chinese fashion and greets Chin by saying, "Many things."

A number of significant events are involved in this interaction that point to a developing creole sensibility. First, Allwyn is impressed by the effort that Chin has put into decorating the shop for Christmas. He sees that Chin is trying to share in the life of the community. Second, Allwyn is, for the first time, actually close to Chin's wife and is struck by her beauty. This sense of nearness between cultures is at the heart of theories on creolization, for it is the close proximity of cultures that allows for an appreciation of their different aspects that facilitates and fosters cultural exchanges. In the end, this moment becomes a powerful image of such cross-cultural interchange: the Christmas decorations surrounding the "foreign" Chinese and the words of a "foreign" holiday greeting in the mouth of a West Indian boy at Christmas time.

Like the contact facilitated by the shop, a shared educational system has also long been understood to be an important means of developing national solidarity because the shared curriculum, language, and rituals in the classroom create a common culture for students.[24] Thus, it is perhaps unsurprising that West Indian literature often depicts the classroom, particularly when associated with a Chinese character, as a crucible within which broadly inclusive boundaries of national belonging can be established. In *Bound for Trinidad,* by Helen Atteck, for example, Wu Li's first day of school takes on such significance. At the end of the day, Wu Li's budding friendship with a classmate named Martin is interrupted when Martin's mother rudely throws the biscuit that Wu Li has shared with Martin on the ground and then hurries her son away. Despite her apparently racist actions, the possibility—or perhaps, the inevitability—of the development of a more ethnically inclusive sense of community is recognized when Chan reacts to the incident by simply commenting: "If only the adults would not interfere, the children would break down the formalities, and this would be a much more harmonious society."[25]

The significance of school space to the development of creole culture is demonstrated more fully in *A Brighter Sun* when Tall Boy sends his children to school for the first time. Upon their appearance in the schoolyard, the children are greeted with the refrain: "Chinee, Chinee never die/ Flat nose and chinky eye!" Not intimidated, the children respond with racial insults of their own: "Nigger is ah nation/ Dey full of bodderation/ Meet dem by de station/ Dey stink wid perspiration." Then, turning to the Indo-Trinidadian children in the crowd, they announce: "Everybody know allyu does use ah bottle of water in de w.c." The schoolyard then disintegrates into a cacophony of ethnic insults: "Chinese does eat cat an' dog!" "Nigger does smell stink wid perspiration!" "Coolie people does eat wid dey hands!" "Whitey cockroach!" and "Black tar-baby!"[26]

The importance of this scene for affirming a creole narrative of identity is threefold. First, it shows that the Chinese communities are well ensconced within Trinidad's tension-filled spaces of ethnic contact. After all, the fact that the Chinese children are well aware of the racial insults and slurs to use when addressing members of other ethnic groups in the community demonstrates that they share a common knowledge and representational system (albeit in terms of stereotypes) with the rest of the children in the community. Similarly, Tall Boy's children are also depicted as speaking in the same creole style as the rest of their classmates. Their language use does not identify them as outsiders; rather, it demonstrates that they share not only a common knowledge, but a common language with the rest of the villagers. Finally, *A Brighter Sun* ultimately asserts Selvon's belief in the ability of Trinidadians to transcend their ethnic differences and create an inclusive sense of community. The schoolyard incident recognizes the ethnic mélange that exists in Trinidad and the discord that sometimes exists when various groups come in contact with one another. But the fact that this episode takes place in a schoolyard and among children is highly significant; for, in the next scene, the children are shown sitting quietly, side-by-side doing their schoolwork. The scene suggests that despite the obvious ethnic differences among Trinidadians, their shared educational experience somehow overrides these disparities and creates a new sense of community found in a common purpose and an ability to work together. By focusing on Tall Boy's children in this episode, Selvon includes the Chinese community firmly within this vision of a new, inclusive Trinidadian society. Indeed, the presence of members of the minority Chinese population in such scenes becomes a powerful means of affirming the very existence of this shared culture.[27]

The use of a Chinese character as a means of highlighting the important role that the school plays as a site of contact between ethnic groups that precedes the creation of a common culture is a strategy that is also used in Alecia McKenzie's short story "The Grenada Defense League" and in Mittelholzer's *A Morning in the Office*. In a manner reminiscent of Naipaul's *Guerrillas*, "The Grenada Defense League" exposes a shallow and uncommitted attitude toward true revolutionary change in the West Indies when a group of middle-class university students—whose friendships were formed in high school—decides that it will fight American imperialism in Grenada by sailing to the island on a small fishing boat, armed with nothing but machetes. McKenzie specifically includes a Chinese Jamaican named Sonny in the group of would-be revolutionaries as a means of underscoring that this arrogant ignorance is shared among this generation of his social class regardless of ethnic background. Indeed, Sonny is depicted as being so like the rest of the group members in this regard that when the rasta who is supposed to provide them with guns and military training asks suspiciously, "Who the Chinee man? . . . It took them a moment to realize that he meant Sonny, and it took Sonny even longer to realize Faddo was referring to him."[28]

In *A Morning in the Office*, Mittelholzer explores the pervasive class and other social biases that are enmeshed in Trinidadian culture through the interactions of a group of office workers who are drawn from the broadest spectrum of Trinidadian society. Among them is Olga Yen Tip, who, despite the small freedoms from social convention that she is allowed as discussed in the previous chapter, generally understands and maintains the prejudices of her society, particularly in relation to social class hierarchies. For example, Olga always addresses the White assistant manager in the office as "Sir," indicating that she recognizes her lower social status. In contrast, both Miss Henery and Mrs. Hinckson, upper middle-class coloreds, insist on addressing him by his name, Mr. Murrain, to demonstrate that they do not consider him to be their social superior. At the same time, Olga understands that she is in a higher social class than the Black office boy; thus, she shows him little deference, greeting him simply by his last name. Olga's behavior is related to the fact that she, like the rest of her family who are long-term residents of Trinidad, has developed a British West Indian "outlook" which is rooted in her education: "Together with her negro, East Indian, Portuguese, Spanish and colored school companions, [Olga] had grown up with the *Royal Reader, Gentle Jesus, meek and mild*, Sir Walter Scott and *Drink to me only with thine eyes.*"[29] In this description, it is clear that school is not simply a site where facts are learned; rather it is the location in which various ethnicities meet, develop, and learn accepted social conventions.

"A Mix-up Country": Confirming "Creoleness"

The fictional representations of the Chinese shop and the village school are not only exemplary sites in which to locate Hall's "*Terra Incognita*," that "'New World' . . . ground, place, territory . . . where strangers from every other part of the globe [collide]" and act out "creoleness"; they are also important locations from which to resist the historical "silences" and "suppressions" that Hall warns can easily occur when "trying to represent a diverse people with a diverse history" even within the context of creole identities.[30] Indeed, Hall is only too conscious of this danger when he admits that he has collapsed "the many other cultural 'presences' that constitute the complexity of Caribbean identity (Indian, Chinese, Lebanese, etc.)" in his attempt to formulate a theory of Caribbean diaspora.[31] Particularly in recent fiction from the West Indies, however, authors have made conscious efforts to acknowledge that the ethnic makeup of the region comprises more than the descendants of Africans and Europeans—of making the attempt, as one character might put it, to give a voice to the people "on all dem ship from China, from India, from Africa" who migrated to the West Indies.[32] As work that challenges traditional historical narratives, such fiction becomes an important part of the process of performing belonging within the framework of a creole narrative. National identities are always integrally intertwined with national histories. Indeed, in many ways, national histories exist to produce national identities. "Writing in" the presence of ethnic minorities such as the Chinese into West Indian national histories is therefore a powerful means of recognizing the profound "heterogeneity and diversity" of West Indian cultural identities and thereby affirming a creole narrative.[33]

One of the earliest attempts to incorporate a Chinese presence in Trinidadian history occurs in *A Brighter Sun* when Selvon interrupts the plot midway through the novel to insert a chapter on Chinese Trinidadians that bears little relevance to the overall story line. The chapter is basically a somewhat awkwardly executed attempt to figuratively and literally bring the Chinese in from the margins of Trinidad's "story" by acknowledging their presence and participation in Trinidadian society. Powell's integration of Chinese Jamaican history in *The Pagoda* occurs in a smoother, albeit also subtler, fashion. This subtlety is unsurprising as the novel is not particularly focused on recounting history per se. Nevertheless, Powell effectively captures the loneliness, hard work, and hostility that faced early Chinese Jamaican migrants in brief but powerful comments, such as when

Lowe notes that legislative measures to restrict Chinese migration to the island are under consideration.

Bound for Trinidad: An Historical Novel, by Helen Atteck, is, as its subtitle indicates, an explicitly historical novel. It traces the story of Cricket, a Hakka woman, from China, through her journey to Trinidad, and ends when her family is securely established in the island. In straightforward fashion, it draws attention to the major events and experiences pertaining to nineteenth-century Chinese migration to the West Indies: the political upheavals in China (most specifically, in this case, the Tai Ping Revolution), that drove so many to consider leaving the country; the coercion and kidnapping that surrounded some of the "decisions" to migrate; the arduous sea journey to the new world; the hardships of indenture; the racism faced by the new migrants; and the slow, but steady progress that they made in setting down roots for their families and securing financial viability. In this sense, *Bound for Trinidad* is a typical "pioneer story," that is, a historical tale that celebrates the achievements of the founders of the nation. As such, it makes a claim for a more complex and creole understanding of the nation by deeming the Chinese to be one group of Trinidadian pioneers.

Perhaps what is as yet the most beautifully rendered fictional exploration of West Indian history to specifically incorporate the Chinese is Margaret Cezair-Thompson's novel *The True History of Paradise.* Set in Jamaica in the early 1980s, a period of extreme political turbulence and violence (indeed, the story takes place during a state of emergency), the novel describes the flight of a young woman, Jean, as she traverses the island from one end to the other to reach an airport from which she will escape the horrifying bloodshed that is washing over the country. Along the way, Jean recounts the personal events that have led her to make the drastic choice to leave the island. But the story she tells is not hers alone. "Ghosts stand on the foothills of this journey . . . obstinate spirits, desperate to speak"; and speak they do.[34] At various points on the journey, often when Jean reaches landmarks that correspond with significant historical events such as the site of the earthquake that destroyed Port Royal in the eighteenth century or the location of the 1865 Morant Bay Rebellion, Jean's long-dead ancestors and other deceased family members literally insert themselves into the text to tell their stories. By the end of the novel, their stories have mixed with Jean's own personal narrative to provide a broad historical context for her decision to leave and to construct a complex depiction of Jamaican history as both "a history of hell . . . [and] a history of grace terrestrial."[35]

Jean's ancestors are "Africans . . . English, Irish, Spanish, Jewish, Germans, and Chinese."[36] Her personal life is also filled with people who represent other ethnic groups on the island, such as Mark, the man of Lebanese and Portuguese descent whom she dates, the imaginary Arawak friend she had as a child, and her half-sister, whose father is Indian. As such, the Jamaica that Jean encounters in her family and on her journey not only has the potential of being of creole—that is, has the component ethnic parts that can be melded together—it is already creolized. Indeed, the corporate history that emerges from the chorus of voices to become the novel's tale is as much a creole expression of this "mix-up country" as it is an act of creolization.[37]

The connection between the presence of the Chinese and the existence of a creole community established by the historical narratives is suggested by the important role given to the character Cherry Ho Sing Landing. Cherry personifies all aspects of what is generally understood to mean creole in the West Indies: she is the progeny of a Chinese man and Black Jamaican woman and she functions in an environment of cultural mixing evidenced, for example, by her use of Jamaican patois or the fact that her Christmas dinner combines dishes from African, European, and Chinese cuisines. More important, Cherry is "the family matriarch" and the "head of the family," which is itself a symbol of the nation.[38] She is, in other words, placed at the center of the nation. Her significance is also indicated by the fact that she is the one who deals with some of the family's most difficult situations, such as opening her home to Jean when her parents briefly separate, being the only one brave enough to tell Jean's mother, Monica, that her daughter, Lana, has become pregnant, and convincing Lana that it would be in her son's best interest to migrate out of Jamaica with his aunt. Cherry is also depicted as being as deeply rooted in the greater national community as she is in her own family. She never shows any desire to leave Jamaica, even as conditions become more and more dangerous. The very fact that she is eventually held up at gunpoint indicates how Jamaican she is, for like the rest of the individuals in the country, she does not remain unscathed by the violence.

Mr. Ho Sing, Cherry's father, migrated from China as an indentured laborer in the nineteenth century. He appears only twice in the novel; first, on his deathbed and, second, as one of the "dreamed speakers of an earlier world" whose stories meld with Jean's to reconstruct Jamaican history.[39] Both appearances are, however, important in terms of indicating a banalized understanding of belonging that is based on a creole articulation of nation. First, as his death scene occurs on some of the earliest pages of the novel, Mr. Ho Sing gets priority of attention from the reader. He is far from being a marginal presence. Second, his early appearance in the text, brief as it is, disrupts any assumptions of Jamaica as a "Black" nation with which the reader may have begun the text. In this regard, it is also significant that he is the ancestor of such a large number of Jamaicans (Jean suggests that his descendants number close to a hundred) who are represented as being essentially creole in their makeup in that they exist in "varying shades of white, yellow, and brown faces—the mixed-up progeny of the old man's oceanic urges."[40] Third, like his daughter, Mr. Ho Sing is depicted as being firmly rooted in Jamaica when, on his deathbed, he continues to speak in Jamaican patois instead of reverting to Chinese. That this creole language has become his "native tongue" signifies that Jamaica is truly home space for Mr. Ho Sing.

The personal history of his migration and life on the island, which Mr. Ho Sing relates to Jean in "ghost form," also validates the history of the Chinese in Jamaica and pushes back the narrative boundaries of nation to include them. In the telling of his story, the experience of Chinese indenture and shopkeeping moves from the footnotes of Jamaican history to center stage. Not only does Mr. Ho Sing's story refocus the historical lens; it also rewrites the traditionally understood history of hostile Chinese-Black relations in Jamaica when he reminds the reader that the 1918 uprising against Chinese shopkeepers was the result of a personal feud between a Chinese shopkeeper and a Black man over a woman.[41] In fact, not only does Mr. Ho Sing disrupt the historical narrative that interprets the incident as evidence of Black-Chinese hostility, he also rewrites history when he asserts: "Dem say Black people turn against Chinee shopkeeper. So dem say, dem history book an' history teacher. But is not true. Syrian shop-dem don't give credit to Black people. Only Chinee give credit and sell small-small fe Black people. Is not true dem hate we."[42] Thus Mr. Ho Sing directly challenges historical narratives that depict the Chinese simply as despised outsiders to the nation.

A Mangrove Existence: The Entanglements of a Creole Life

In pointing to a difference in business practice between Syrian and Chinese shopkeepers, Mr. Ho Sing suggests that the Chinese shopkeepers understand well the lives of their Black customers. The granting of goods by "trusting" and the willingness to sell items in extremely small amounts (like selling one or two cigarettes rather than the whole pack) establish bonds between Blacks and Chinese that also serve as the building blocks for shared cultural practices between the two groups. Simply put, the two groups share a way of living. Fiction that portrays the Chinese as sharing the experiences and perspectives of other West Indians is a particularly important strategy for demonstrating the existence of a creole community and identity. Additionally, such representation also demonstrates exactly which norms and values are deemed to be "West Indian."

It would be difficult, if not impossible, to argue that dealing with the destructive legacy of colonialism has not been the overriding experience of West Indians. In Selvon's *Turn Again Tiger*, a struggle to survive the devastating aftereffects of colonialism is revealed to impact the entire community through the parallel experiences of Tiger and the Chinese shopkeeper, Otto. The title character, Tiger, a symbol of the young nation, must come to grips with the history of Indian indenture before he and, on a symbolic level, the nation can reach maturity. Specifically, Tiger must come to terms with his fears, self-loathing, and feelings of powerlessness. The violent sexual encounter between Tiger and the White manager's wife in the cane fields becomes the moment in which Tiger symbolically grapples with, and overcomes, his indentured labor history. Just as Tiger must come to grips with the history of the Indians in the cane fields, Otto must also address the similar history of the Chinese in Trinidad.

Like the Indians, the Chinese were brought to Trinidad originally as indentured laborers; and in the cane fields, they faced the same conditions as the Indians and the Africans before them—conditions designed to debase and deny their humanity. It is therefore no accident that the ultimate negation of Otto's manhood takes place in the cane field—it is where his wife, Berta, carries on her affair with one of the cane cutters. Thus it is that, like Tiger, it is in the cane fields that Otto must reclaim his manhood. This occurs when Otto finally comes out from behind the counter and fights his wife's lover amid the cane. It is only after engaging in this struggle that Berta, her lover, and the community at large finally see Otto as a man rather than as a somewhat marginal comic buffoon and Otto's acceptance in the village becomes complete. In this acceptance, one sees defined a creole version of history that validates Chinese and Indian experiences as part of the development of a confident and secure sense of nationhood.

Otto and Tiger's journey is, in many ways, a quest to reclaim the power that was stripped from their communities as part of the debasement inherent in the colonial experience. As such, *Turn*

Again Tiger has much in common with the hauntingly beautiful novel *Bruised Hibiscus*, by Elizabeth Nunez. This novel, also set in Trinidad, begins with the discovery of a brutally murdered woman. This is, however, "no ordinary woman." Instead she is

> a white woman; the kind of woman who, to the eyes of the villagers, seemed mystically protected, unaffected by the taint of poverty, sickness or the everyday tide of calamities taken as a way of life in Otahiti; protected certainly from the vulgarity of violence . . . to see one now, dead, a lump of flesh, rotting, corbeaux screeching, ready to pounce from between the rusty edges of wind-torn sea-almond leaves, there must be meaning.[43]

What is exposed with the body of the dead woman—the meaning of her death, so to speak—is the continuing existence of a colonial will to power through the degradation, humiliation, and destruction of others that saturates their society. Whether one is a "White" Trinidadian descended from the land-owning classes, a middle-class intellectual, an individual raised in the slums of Lavantille or in a Chinese shop—no one is immune; no one is safe. In this regard, the description of the young men in Chinaman's shop applies to the country as a whole: they have

> lost [the] capacity to express any emotion except derision, their mirthless laughter always ready to disavow the serious, to diminish the beautiful. These were [people] prematurely forged into cynics by deprivation and failure or rather by the loss of faith in the possibility of the reversal of their misfortunes; [people] who, having nowhere to go, sought to build colonies of their kind if only through the debasement of others.[44]

That the White woman is killed despite the colonial power structures of the island meant to keep a woman in her position inviolate only reemphasizes how widespread this destructive desire is. That the Chinaman also shares this attitude serves a similar literary purpose.

The colonial relationship between colonizer and colonized is essentially one of crushing domination on the part of the colonizer. In the novel, those who have suffered from such domination seek, in turn, to position themselves as colonizers in other relationships in their lives. This desire and its horrifying effects are explored by Nunez through "man-woman business"—namely through the poisonous marriages of Rosa and Cedric, and Zuela and the Chinaman.[45]

Using "man-woman business" as an analogy of the colonial relationship has a particularly long tradition in West Indian literature. Indeed, *Bruised Hibiscus* draws consciously on Jean Rhys's important postcolonial novel *Wide Sargasso Sea* in its depiction of the destructive relationship between White creole Rosa, her "Brown" husband Cedric, and her nurse, Mary Christophe. On first reading, the relationship between Zuela and the Chinaman may also seem familiar. But the Chinaman of *Bruised Hibiscus* is radically different from those of other "Chinamen" who populate West Indian literature in that Nunez provides the reader with his background as a means of explaining his behavior. He is no longer presented as being innately cruel and sinister by racial default; instead, his abusive treatment of Zuela is revealed to be one of the means by which he tries to alleviate the searing sense of guilt that he suffers over the deaths of his wife and daughter in China. Their deaths were extracted by his villagers as the price for his participation in the illegal opium trade, a trade that was part of British imperial aggression in the region. The specific historical context in which Nunez places the death of his family situates the Chinaman in the midst of the same colonial forces that shape Trinidad. The Chinaman's reaction to that experience is the same as that of other Trinidadians: the pursuit of a grasping desire for colonizing domination, expressed in his relationship to Zuela. As Rosa sums it up in her comparison of her and Zuela's marriages, their experiences are "The same. . . . No different."[46] In this way, her words become a very succinct statement on the "West Indianness" of the Chinaman's experiences throughout the novel and identify him as belonging in this society.

Like Chinaman of *Bruised Hibiscus*, Chinese shopkeepers are often afforded a key role in revealing the common life experiences and cultural values at play in West Indian communities. In the short story "Wing's Way," by Noel Woodroffe, the Chinese shopkeeper lives a life as defined by poverty as that of the other villagers. Indeed, he is as trapped in the village as the flamingo that is arrested in flight from the mangrove in the picture to which he is so attached. In the short story "The Beauty Contest" and the play "Highway in the Sun," a reworking of Selvon's novel *Turn Again Tiger*, the representation of the Chinese shopkeeper also draws attention to the pervasiveness of one aspect of West Indian experience, namely, the breakdown of a sense of community in a post–World War II society. "The Beauty Contest" explores this transition by focusing on a business competition between Mr. Prasad and Mr. Aleong, owners of the two hardware shops in Doon Town. The two had coexisted peacefully for years, but their easy relationship is strained when Aleong's son returns from studying business abroad and begins to make changes to his father's shop. His behavior results in a business competition that culminates when each businessman sponsors his own contestant in a local beauty competition.

"Highway in the Sun" notes a similar development of a selfish individualism as marking Trinidadian experience in this period. This attitude is revealed when Joe constantly tells Tiger to leave him out of things, in Boysie's desperate desire to leave Trinidad to make more money, and in the two doctors' refusals to help Urmilla during her difficult labor. The idea that this rampant self-interest has permeated all levels of society is given further credence when even Tall Boy is portrayed as being affected by this mood of "every man for himself."[47] Tall Boy is represented as turning his back on the old communal way of village life when he builds a partition in his shop, separating the American GIs from the locals, and providing the soldiers with better service because, in his words, "I know which side my bread butter."[48]

Other examples of the use of Chinese characters to identify shared cultural values and norms range from the subtle, such as, when the narrator of "Jakes Makes" wants to demonstrate her rebellion against middle-class attitudes by becoming a Buddhist, noting that "*even the Chinese* in my class were the staunchest of Catholics" (emphasis added), to the more explicit, such as the depiction of the assimilated Chinese family, the Grangers, in *A Morning in the Office*, or Wilson Harris' inclusion of Chinese characters in his imagined landscapes of Guyana.[49] Indeed, at times the Chinese communities of the West Indies are represented as being so enmeshed in West Indian life that they actually become powerful symbols of conventional West Indian values. This device is particularly apparent in Paule Marshall's short story "British Guiana" and N. D. Williams' novel *Ikael Torass*.

"British Guiana" recounts the last day in the life of Motley, a member of the Guyanese fair-skinned and privileged upper class. Although Motley seemed destined to follow the social path set out for him by the class into which he was born, the story reveals that his public persona is at odds with his true self. After all, Motley hangs out at a bar that caters to social outcasts, "the idle . . . the cheap thieves and cozners, the panderers . . . the brawlers."[50] Motley also indulges in other behavior that deviates from the norms of his class; these include his attempt to lead the stevedores on strike, his long-term affair with Sybil, a part-Chinese woman, and his obvious homosexual attraction to Sidney.

The story hangs on the question of whether Motley will ever be true to himself. The deciding moment for Motley comes when he is offered a job with BG Broadcasting, a job that would, in effect, secure his place within the upper middle-class establishment. Before he decides whether to take the job, Motley and Sybil go on a trip into the bush. Alone in the jungle, the bush "closed around him, becoming another dimension of himself, the self he had long sought. For the first time this self was within his grasp. If he pursued this dark way long enough he would find it . . . and it would either shape his life . . . or destroy him."[51] Before Motley can pursue this path to self-discovery, however, Sybil comes upon him. She immediately understands that if Motley were to choose "the bush," he would destroy his public persona and all the status and privileges that come with it. Sybil's response is to rush forward "[w]ith a protective cry . . . and [place] herself between him and what could have been a vision of himself."[52] By placing herself between Motley and "the bush," Sybil becomes the personification of the class norms and values that block Motley from truly seeing and knowing himself. Ultimately, this destines him to physical and emotional death.

In a similar fashion, Precious, the part-Chinese woman with whom the narrator of *Ikael Torass* embarks on a brief affair, is represented in such a manner that she becomes the personification of the middle-class West Indian value system that the narrator eventually rejects. As a member of "the Octaroons," a group of fair-skinned women on campus who hold themselves aloof from other students, particularly those who are politically active, Precious is depicted as being distanced from the interests of the Black masses. Her distance from the events that touch these young people is not attributed to the fact that she has Chinese ancestry; rather, it is made clear that she is alienated from their interests because she is secure as a member of the colored upper and middle classes who oppose any "Africanization" of their nation in their attempts to hold on to British colonial values and hierarchies. Thus, Precious does not participate in the student protest and is, significantly, depicted at the conclusion of the novel tending to a sick Norwegian rather than caring about the welfare of her fellow Black citizens.

Precious' attitude points to another West Indian value that is often explored through depictions of Chineseness, namely, a denigration of "Africanness." Many contemporary West Indian authors struggle with what they perceive to be a West Indian rejection of its African heritage as invalid and shameful. One of the ways in which authors draw attention to this attitude is to contrast how West Indian communities so readily accept Chinese features as being acceptable as a standard of beauty while rejecting African features. In a manner that is similar to the means by which the Chinese are used to define an ultimate outer barrier to West Indian spaces, this contrast suggests that the rejection of an African heritage in the West Indies is so absolute that *even* Chinese features are deemed more beautiful than African ones.

In "Jakes Makes," a critique of Jamaican society's inability to appreciate its African heritage is symbolized by the community's rejection of Jakes and his art. Jakes is considered a rebel in the neighborhood partially because he is "proud of his broad nose, his wide mouth and his course hair" and of the fact that "he had not a drop of anything besides African blood."[53] Similarly, Jakes' attraction to Grace is largely due to the fact that she had the same "deep black skin as Jakes. Her color was perhaps the thing that most attracted Jakes."[54] The fact that Jakes' "Black pride" seems odd to his neighbors is used by McKenzie to demonstrate just how deep-seated is their rejection of their African heritage, particularly when this rejection is placed against how quickly the community is to deem Clarissa, Grace's part-Chinese daughter, as beautiful. In fact, Clarissa's features are so readily accepted and valued by Jamaicans in general that she is represented as winning beauty contests when she becomes a teenager.[55]

The same valuation of Chinese features that suggests an overall devaluation of "Africanness" in the West Indies is also evident in Mendes' work, albeit somewhat subconsciously, and, more explicitly in *Ikael Torass.* In both Mendes' short story "Her Chinaman's Way" and the novel *Pitch Lake*, the women who are deemed to be beautiful are of a mixed ethnic heritage that includes a Chinese background. In *Pitch Lake*, the novel's tragic Portuguese hero has affairs only with women who cannot be defined as Black in terms of an African appearance, such as the brown-skinned maid of an indeterminate ethnic background and Maria, the part-Chinese girl from the barrack-yard. In contrast, Blackness is represented as having no value in terms of beauty. Thus, the Black cook Rebecca, despite being one of the kindest people in the text, is described in the most unflattering of terms: " . . . obese . . . her large bust like a pillow within her bodice, her face hideous with its black skin, everted lips, splayed nose and small insidious eyes."[56] In "Her Chinaman's Way," Mendes makes a similar contrast between Maria, who with "Chinese blood in her veins . . . had always been sought after by the men in town," and Philogen, who is described simply as "gaunt, ugly and black."[57]

In an analogous fashion, Chinese features are so valued in *Ikael Torass* as a mark of beauty specifically because they are not African that they become a status symbol. Precious' acceptance into "the Octaroon" clique is directly related to the fact that her Chinese ancestry is more apparent than her Maroon heritage. This is made clear by the hostile reaction of her friends to her relationship with the narrator. Their disapproval is based largely on the fact that he is a "[t]otal *dark* stranger" (emphasis added).[58] A valuation of Chinese features over African ones is again suggested in "British Guiana," where Sybil and her sister's rise in social and economic status is not affected by their appearance. In contrast, Sidney attributes part of his failure to advance socially to the fact that "I don't look white. My father and his father were like so.' He raised a dark angry hand."[59]

Ultimately, fictional images that portray the Chinese as being increasingly embedded in a cultural space that transforms itself to accommodate their presence points to the development and existence of a unique, fluid, local culture from which ideas of an ethnically and culturally inclusive national identity organically emerge. The sense of change and transformation, that is, of creolization, that is inherent in such a concept accounts for the images of gaps between "home-born" and "local-born" Chinese that abound throughout West Indian literature: in "The Grenada Defense League," Sonny's parents would prefer that he date a Chinese girl, but Sonny disregards their wishes to chase after a Black Jamaican girl; in *A Morning in the Office*, Olga and her immediate family had lived so long in Trinidad that they have no knowledge of any Chinese language and are described as being barred from a Chinese "mindset"; in *The Pagoda*, not only does Lowe's daughter marry a Black Jamaican, she retains no Chinese language or cultural traits at all; and in "Wing's Way," Wing's children neither participate in nor understand their father's exercises and speak "imperfect, halting Chinese."[60]

The Hills of Hebron goes even further in showing the failure of the China-born Chinese to distance their local-born children from their West Indian communities. Chin-Quee tries desperately to keep his daughter from the rest of the villagers when as a youngster she is prohibited from playing "with children of an *alien race*" (emphasis added).[61] She is given a Chinese name, even though her mother is Black and, once she hits puberty, she is kept in the shop to ensure that she does not mix with any of the village men. Nevertheless, Chin-Quee ultimately fails at separating his daughter from the village. No one, including Chin-Quee, calls her by her Chinese name and her awareness of the local song about Moses' failed ascension demonstrates that she has access to village folklore and gossip. More significant, in the end, she becomes the mother of Rose Brown, the character who becomes the symbol of hope and the future for the people of Hebron. As such, she is fundamentally as much a member of what her China-born father deems an "alien race" as anyone else in the community. Moreover, she not only belongs to the community; through her pregnancy, she helps create it.

The representation of Chinese characters in West Indian literature as participating in, and contributing to the local community challenges

> the unrealistic claims of homogenizing nationalistic projects and the simplism of the binary logic (such as black-white or Creole-indigenous) through which many nationalistic discourses in Latin America and the Caribbean have been constructed. . . . Ultimately [the presence of the Chinese] redirect[s] the domain of . . . ethnicity toward the notion of cultural difference and place it above [limited] nationalistic claims.[62]

Such images speak to a well-established belief in the existence and validity of cultural difference in the West Indies despite other narratives that purport more limited renderings of nation.

The association between the Chinese and creolization that is asserted in literary images is as much a part of the performance of a creole national identity as are official state articulations of creolization such as those found in national anthems, mottoes, or histories.

These representations also point to an understanding of belonging as something that is "subject to the continuous 'play' of history, culture, and power."[63] In *The True History of Paradise,* Mr. Ho Sing's narrative draws attention to the inevitable instability of boundaries that are set within creole understandings of identity when he describes his journey from China to Jamaica in the following terms: "Wha' people dem suffer on all dem ship . . . nobody know, nobody can say. Too much people. Too much story."[64] Clearly, this narrative silence is not the silence of marginalization but points to the failure of language to adequately describe the events that he lived through. Even more important, however, his statement points to the impossibility of claiming closure for national narratives because there is simply "too much story" to be told, and by extension, many ways of performing belonging. In the next chapter, I explore some of these other stories in the examination of how Chinese West Indian authors work through the ambiguity of belonging in their representation of Chineseness.

4 / From the Other Side of the Counter: Chinese West Indian Self-Representations

Friends talk
And they laugh
Because you 'born and grow'
Behind the counter.

—EASTON LEE, "ALL WEEK"

The readiness with which images of the Chinese have been used as boundary markers in West Indian national narratives of oppression and creoleness can be partially attributed to the visibility of Chinese ethnicity in the West. In other words, it is not that "being Chinese" somehow makes this ethnic group particularly suited to define the boundaries of nation; rather, their visible difference from the more numerically dominant sectors of West Indian populations, combined with their minority status, makes it both easy and attractive to imagine them in this symbolic role. In "The Fact of Blackness," Frantz Fanon noted a similar phenomenon pertaining to African features in the West. Fanon argued that African features—"Blackness"—are read as visual codes that purportedly define how those who bear them are to conduct themselves, to perceive the world around them, and, in turn, how the world reacts to them. Thus, Fanon concluded that although Blackness is a physical reality, it is also the necessary condition to an imposed identity (that is, a space of belonging) that is woven "out of a thousand details, anecdotes, stories" by a White Other such that "not only must the black man be black, he must be black in relation to the white man."[1]

For Fanon, the successful imposition of this identity is connected to the fact that it is "triggered" by an obvious visual stimulus—Blackness. In his illustration of the White Parisian child's encounter with a Black man, the moment of identification—"look mother, a Negro"—is also the moment when the Black identity is imposed on the Black man. The theorist Ien Ang suggests a similar connection between visibility and an imposed identity for Chinese in the West when she recounts the moment when a Chinese Australian was called a "Ching Chong Chinaman" in a schoolyard incident. Like Fanon, Ang points out that this moment relies on the recognition of difference; that is, it "depended on the availability of some clues that enabled him to single out the guileless William as an appropriate object of such an attack: What else could it have been but his 'yellow skin' and 'slanty eyes,' the key 'racial' markers for Chineseness in the West?"[2]

The correlation between racialization and the imposition of a limited identity for the Chinese has been recognized in a number of West Indian literary texts. In Robert Standish's *Mr. On Loong*, despite the fact that John grows up almost entirely removed from Chinese cultural influences, "by upbringing and training less Chinese than an Englishman or a Frenchman," like "a neglected rose-bush reverting to the wild rambler, impelled by the law which seems to force every living creature or plant, in the absence of some strong counter-influence, to revert to its parent type," he grows up to exhibit the traits that Standish deems to be integrally Chinese.[3] In Powell's *The Pagoda*, the story's tension lies in Lowe's struggle to free himself from the "the fabulous masquerade that was his life," including being outfitted as a Chinese shopkeeper by Cecil. Indeed, Cecil not only replaces Lowe's clothes, he also gives Lowe a stage and a backdrop against which to act out his new identity when he sets Lowe up in a shop.[4] That the villagers often simply call Lowe by the generic "Mr. Chin," a name that they apparently give to all the Chinese shopkeepers on the island, also points to the limitations inherent in Lowe's racialized identity. Naipaul also explicitly addresses the limitations of ethnic racialization in "The Baker's Story," when, to be successful, a Black baker must provide a "Chinese face" for his business. The story hangs on an ironic reversal of the seemingly inclusive claim in Trinidad's national anthem that there is a place for every creed and race in Trinidad by showing a world in which "every race have to do special things"; that is, where race places the individual in specified socioeconomic spaces.[5] In the Trinidad depicted in the story, the baked goods sector of the economy has been designated as "Chinese space." Thus, the bakery essentially becomes a stage in which a form of Chineseness is acted out complete with appropriate props; namely, a store sign and newspapers written in Chinese calligraphy, and a "Chinese-looking" employee, complete with a fake Chinese accent, serving at the counter.

As with all the literature examined so far, however, such work is not written by Chinese West Indians. This chapter asks the obvious question: How do the literary representations of Chinese West Indians *by* Chinese West Indians affect the depictions of the relationship between Chineseness and nation? Is the ambiguity of belonging stabilized or does it become even more overt? Does the multiplicity of national narratives increase? Does such writing challenge popular conceptions of the Chinese or does it, to paraphrase Fanon, simply stay within the imaginative bounds set out for it? Simply put, what happens when Chineseness is constructed from the other side of the counter?

Before beginning to address these questions, it is necessary to note the relative paucity of texts available for such study. Currently, there are very few authors of Chinese West Indian descent who are publishing their work. To further compound this difficulty, those who are writing, are not necessarily concerned with interrogating representations of Chinese West Indians. Perhaps most noticeable in this regard is the work of Willi Chen whose two collections of short stories, *King of the Carnival* and *Chutney Power*, contain no major Chinese character. Similarly, only two of Meiling Jin's short stories in her collection *Song of the Boatwoman* specifically explore the experiences of Chinese West Indians.

It is difficult to account for this seeming lack of interest in expressing Chinese West Indian voices and visions.[6] Chen suggests that his writing is heavily affected by the very real fact that Indo- and Afro-Trinidadians dominate the population of Trinidad and Tobago numerically. He claims that this reality has directly influenced his choice of what and whom he writes about.[7] Easton Lee suggests different reasons for Chinese West Indians' literary silence.[8] First, he points to a language issue. Traditionally, English was not the first language or even a comfortable mode of expression for many Chinese West Indians. Anything written in Chinese, however, was largely inaccessible to an English-reading public. This reality created very practical barriers for potential Chinese West Indian authors in terms of developing a wide reading public and for getting published. Second, Lee suggests that the Chinese in the West Indies were, as a minority population, "made to feel ashamed" of those aspects of their culture and experiences that differed from those of the more dominant West Indian culture(s) within which they lived. He suggests that the political and cultural marginalization of the Chinese communities of the West Indies might have sent them the message that other West Indians would not have any interest in what the Chinese had to say and that this served as another deterrent to potential Chinese West Indian authors.

Although such factors may have contributed to the makings of a small pool of work from which to explore literary self-representation by Chinese West Indians, the literature that is available is by no means insignificant, if not simply by the mere fact that it disturbs the imaginative construct of the West Indies as "Black space." Just as the depictions of Indo-Caribbean communities that appeared in work by internationally acclaimed authors such as V. S. Naipaul and Samuel Selvon added to the understanding of the complex cultural mélange that is the basis of West Indian cultural identities, the authors examined in this chapter have begun an important process: they challenge the reader to reimagine the narratives in which West Indian cultural and national identities have been articulated to include the presence of the Chinese in a more central fashion and, in doing so, challenge the very boundaries of what it means to "be Chinese" and to "be West Indian."

Re-Orienting Alienation

Literary critic David Palumbo-Liu suggests that Asian American self-representation in literature is problematic because the "minority Self" is unable to truly appropriate the symbolic codes of the White Other due to the "overwhelming cultural authority of the Other."[9] He maintains that the "White Other" intervenes into Asian American self-representations because it allows only "certain self-representing signifiers to the minority individual, [and] mediates any coming-into-Being in representation" and provides a reading of two Asian American texts to show how the authors are at times complicit in objectifying Asianness when they subscribe "to the Other's discourse while being absolutely alienated from using it."[10] Liu is primarily interested in exploring the processes behind this self-representation and their effects within the relatively small sphere of literary texts; however, other scholars have been interested in how Asian and Asian American constructions can reify and appropriate Orientalist representations often as a means of asserting a distinctive cultural identity more broadly, a process that has come to be known as "Self-Orientalization."

In his analysis of the poetry and paintings of four Chinese Cuban artists, López-Calvo uses the model of Self-Orientalism as a means of exploring "patterns of essentialization, stereotyping, and dehumanization" of Chineseness in their work.[11] His study reveals that for these artists, Self-Orientalism is largely expressed in depictions of an exoticized, and usually highly romanticized, China. In the literature of Chinese West Indians, however, this idealization of an essentialized Chineseness is largely lacking, although the paean-type celebration of Chinese heritage that exists in Easton Lee's poetry collection *Heritage Call: Ballad for the Children of the Dragon* might be read in this fashion. More commonly, Chinese West Indians reinscribe the Chinese as a "contrasting image"—the outsider and alien—to other West Indians. Nevertheless, the image of Chinese alienation is renegotiated by Chinese West Indian authors such that alienation is not necessarily represented as being inherently antagonistic to other West Indians. In other words, Chinese alienation is not used as a means of marking the outside borders of the nation. Instead, such images are poised on what Liu called "the boundaries of both containment and resistance," which allows them to reveal "the extremely uneven surface of that symbolic and its inherently double nature (at once inclusionary and exclusionary, stable and shifting with regard to its possible subjects)."[12] As a result, the reinscribed image of the alienated Chinese becomes a way of representing Chinese suffering within West Indian spaces. Thus it both confirms the narrative that establishes struggle as the loci of national identity and becomes a means by which to include the Chinese within the boundaries of nation defined in this fashion.

As discussed in Chapter 2, one of the most common tropes of Chineseness in West Indian literature is that of the distanced and disengaged Chinese shopkeeper. This character certainly reappears in the writing of Chinese West Indians. In Victor Chang's autobiographical piece, "Light in the Shop," for example, Chang describes a vast abyss between the customers and his shopkeeper brother when he describes his brother as being "curiously insulated from the life that enters his shop"; "in alien land amid alien people"; and as remaining "curiously detached from the society surrounding" him.[13] Chang is, of course, describing a relatively new migrant to Jamaica, and, as such, this depiction is not surprising; however, there is little indication that this shopkeeper might become less alienated. Instead, the shopkeeper remains fixed in this role when the piece ends with a description of the shopkeeper's room as a fortress or bunker—an image that also suggests that the shopkeeper is at war with the community around him, leaving little hope that the shopkeeper will ever be "at home" in Jamaican space.

Lee marks out a similar space of distance between the Chinese shopkeeper and the local community in the poem "Saturday." Here, however, the shop counter is a point of divide separating the shopkeeper from the vibrant life experiences detailed in the poem. Life takes place on the outer side of the counter, indeed, outside of the shop entirely. In contrast, shop space is depicted as strangely neutralized or cut off from the life outside its door—it is a place where news about life is exchanged, but where life itself is not lived. As if to further emphasize this point, Lee's shopkeeper does not participate in the gossip about village life that takes place within the shop, further removing himself from the life described in the conversation. Community life goes on around and about him, but, like the conversation, the Chinese shopkeeper remains apart from it—the consummate outsider to village life.

Chen is perhaps less consciously reflective of his reinscription of alien status for his Chinese characters. In an interview with Stewart Brown, for example, Chen defines "Trinidad life" as "the Negro life, the Indian life," and the "average Trinidadian" as "the Negro or the Indian."[14] Although Chen is referring to the obvious numeric dominance of these two groups in the general population of Trinidad, his definitions effectively position him and other Chinese Trinidadians outside the boundaries of the term "Trinidadian." In other words, Chinese Trinidadians become something *other than* Trinidadians. This self-imposed alienation is also subtly apparent when Chen, recounting his childhood, remembers how funeral processions would pass his parents' shop. As a sign of respect, his family would close the shop's doors. At that point, Chen recalls, he "used to go and hide and look" at the mourners passing the doors.[15] Although the closure of the shop is an acknowledgment of the funeral, in this memory Chen literally removes himself and his family from the significant events in village life. They become merely distant observers—separated from the community behind doors and windows—rather than active participants in the funeral procession. In a similar fashion, the Chinese characters in Chen's fiction remain predominantly shopkeepers who have little involvement in the goings-on of their communities other than serving at the counter.

Chinese West Indian authors do not, however, simply submit to the "cultural authority of the Other" in depicting the Chinese as aliens. Instead, their writing also challenges the very meaning of Chinese alienation as it is performed in other West Indian texts. This is particularly evident in the way that shop space is depicted. Specifically, Chinese West Indian authors are more apt to recognize that shop space is an environment in which the relationship between the Chinese and other West Indians is never entirely settled; or as Chang recognizes, "[I]t was never a simple or straightforward relationship and it ranged from mutual trust to open antagonism and hostility."[16] When it is depicted as a place of "mutual trust," the image of Chinese shop space as alienated from the interests and desires of other West Indians is subverted. On such occasions, shop space intertwines with village space, thereby opening up the imaginative boundaries of the national community to include the Chinese.

Chang is particularly upfront about the ambiguous nature of relationships in the shop in his piece "Light in the Shop" by drawing attention to a traditional way in which Chinese shopkeepers managed their shops in the West Indies, namely, granting credit to customers—a practice that is significantly known in many areas in the West Indies as "trusting" goods. In this piece, the mutual antagonism between Chang's shopkeeper brother and the broader community around him is disrupted briefly when the brother willingly "trusts" goods to a new customer. Despite the fact that the piece ends with an image of the brother walled up and separated from the community, at the moment of trusting goods, shop space becomes the paradoxical site of "contestation and dependence," and the antagonistic boundary between shopkeeper and villager becomes blurred.[17]

The ambiguous nature of the shopkeeper-villager relationship is also captured in Lee's poem "One Day." Written from the perspective of the customer, the poem humorously suggests that the relationship between the Chinese shopkeeper and the villager is more "love-hate" than "hate-hate." For most of the poem, the narrative voice delivers a series of demanding orders and demeaning insults to the Chinese person serving at the counter. At the moment when the customer is about to leave, however, there is a sudden change of tone when it becomes evident that the purchases will not fit in the customer's basket. At this point, the customer suddenly addresses the shopkeeper with the words: "beg you a paper bag no *me nice fren* . . ." (emphasis added).[18] Although this is the moment on which the humor of the poem hangs, it has greater significance when taken into the context of recurring motifs and themes in Chinese West Indian writing. This moment becomes yet another example of the continuing shifts within the shopkeeper-villager relationship—the continued renegotiation of the boundaries between friend and foe, or enemy and compatriot, that takes place within shop space; for, by calling the shopkeeper "friend," the shopkeeper is drawn into the space of the greater community represented by the customer. He becomes "one of us," and his status as an absolute alien is undermined.

Chinese West Indian authors also wrest control of the image of alienation away from the cultural authority of "the Other" in a radical re-visioning of what it means to be an "alienated Chinese" in the West Indies. For such authors, Chinese shop space is not simply a space that alienates the shopkeeper from that which is without—that is, West Indian creole space—it is also a space that can alienate the shopkeeper from that which is within—his own personal desires, wants, and needs. Indeed, shop space is rewritten so that the shop itself becomes a monstrous entity that is both prisoner and prison to the Chinese shopkeepers. In turn, the Chinese shopkeeper's experience becomes analogous with that of other exploited West Indians, thereby reifying the narrative of oppression for West Indian nationhood at the same time that both the narrative and the concept of nation are expanded to include the Chinese.

In the poems "Friday" and "All Week," Lee presents striking

images of the circumscribed and limited world of the Chinese shopkeeper—a space that is constrained to that which is behind the counter. Such a concept is vividly depicted when the child narrator of "Friday" mourns his inability to participate in those activities that the other children in the community engage in because: "I must be home to take my place/ behind the counter."[18] In "All Week," the narrator observes a similar unhappiness in the young Chinese character's attitude to his enforced separation from his community when the narrator comments, "you watch only from behind/ The counter—/ . . . Friends talk/ And they laugh/ Because you 'born and grow'/ Behind the counter."[19] Chang provides a remarkably similar vision of shop space when he describes his childhood with the words: "[W]e lost out on many a class outing and weekend party; not for us the thrill of a trip to the Peak or to Castleton Gardens, no scout or cadet camps or hiking."[20] Although such images are reminiscent of the depiction of the shopkeeper as distanced from the life of the community produced in other West Indian texts, they are also strikingly different in that they reveal a longing to engage with and participate in life beyond the counter on the part of the Chinese. These images, therefore, disrupt the stereotypical depiction of the alienated Chinese shopkeeper by suggesting that the shopkeepers and their families are not aliens by their own choice; rather, alienation and outsider status are imposed upon them by the lifestyle required to run the shop. It is the shop that imposes itself between the shopkeepers and the villagers, creating a distance with the community that the Chinese would rather bridge.

The Other Side of the Counter

Chinese West Indian authors not only depict shop space as a site that creates alienation, they also rewrite shop space in their explicit designation of the shop as a place of disempowerment for the shopkeeper. One need only remember Meredith's jealousy and resentment toward Jimmy's father in *Guerrillas* to understand how deeply embedded the concept of the Chinese shop as a site of power for the Chinese is in West Indian imaginations to grasp just how radical an act is this reimagining of shop space. The disempowerment, oppression, and exploitation identified with shop space by Chinese West Indian authors appear in many ways. In "Friday" and "Light in the Shop," for example, the shopkeepers cannot respond to the barrage of insults they receive from their customers because they must rely on their customers to survive. The needs of the shop thus take precedence over any need that the shopkeeper might feel to defend him- or herself. On yet another level, the shopkeepers are also subject to the workings of a capitalist system that puts them on a low rung in a chain of profit and exploitation. The shopkeeper is, after all, subject to the vagaries of the marketplace since he must buy his goods from a merchant who is himself trying to make as much profit as he can. The practice of "trusting" goods also places the shopkeeper in a financially vulnerable position because she or he is responsible to pay the merchant for the goods regardless of whether his or her customers pay off their debts. The oppressive nature of shop space for the Chinese shopkeeper and his family is often revealed in little details, such as this memory that Chang recounts: "[F]rom early days we were made to understand that every sweet, every mouthful meant profit lost and so *we were not free* to indulge ourselves" (emphasis added).[22] Similarly, in Lee's poem "Some Days," the shopkeeper's son is reminded by his father that "Money in till look fat/ belong to merchant in town/ member that."[23] Such descriptions construct an image of shop space that is strikingly void of the power and privilege associated with it in other West Indian literature. Indeed, shop space is represented as a place that not only alienates the Chinese but in which they are not free.

By depicting Chinese shop space as a site of dehumanizing exploitation and oppression, Chinese West Indian authors draw on a vivid matrix of imagery that is closely associated with the narratives of slavery and colonial oppression that have played key roles in the construction of national and cultural identities in the West Indies. Drawing on this language and imagery allows Chinese West Indian authors to situate their characters within the discursive framework of slavery that has become central to defining concepts of belonging within the West Indies. In the context of the Chinese shop however, the shopkeeper is represented as a slave, and the shop is depicted as both the slave driver and the field of labor. In this regard, it is also interesting to note that writers such as Chang and Lee refer to the shop on numerous occasions as "the shop" rather than a more personal designation such as "our shop."[24] It is as if these writers are trying not only to create a distance between the shop and the shopkeeper but also to suggest that the shop is a distinct entity with the ability to act against the shopkeeper.

The names of many of Lee's poems in the collection *From Behind the Counter* point to the shopkeeper's life of endless, repetitive drudgery that resonates with a slave lifestyle. "Everyday," "All Week," and the poems named specifically for the days of the week establish a sense of inescapable, monotonous toil for the shopkeeper, as well as a type of physical constraint. In "Everyday," for example, the shopkeeper appears to be as fixed to the space behind the counter as if he had been manacled: "Every morning same time same place/ same ting—/ . . . Like sunrise/ like moon shine/ like sunset."[25] Similarly, in "Next Day," the short, rhythmic lines that describe the activities of the shopkeeper capture the repetitiveness of the actions while suggesting the severely limited nature of the shopkeeper's existence: "wash face—/ make haste—/ open shop—/ watch shop—/ lock shop—/ sweep shop—/ keep shop—/ . . . shop-work it can't done/ for it start all over again/ fore-day morning."[26] In both cases, the shop is depicted as a demanding taskmaster and the shopkeeper represented as his much abused laborer. Significantly, even night does not free the shopkeeper from the shop's oppression. While the villagers are free to return to their homes and rest from their labors, the shopkeeper must remain in the shop to complete preparations for the next day's work. Indeed, so inescapable is the shop that it even seems to follow the shopkeeper to bed, appearing in the scents that linger on his person and invading his very dreams: "[B]rown paper packages/ swim and dance all night around in/ your head" while "You fall asleep/ counting not sheep/ but stacks of paper packages."[27]

Like Lee, Chang represents the shop as a space of oppressive toil, release from which can be found only in flight: "Is it any wonder that we all hated the shop and fled from it as soon as we could?"[28] For Chang, the overriding image of the shop is, in fact, a prison for the shopkeeper and his family. This is suggested in Chang's memories of his childhood where serving the customers is basically equated to serving some kind of punitive sentence. Similarly, his description of the shopkeeper's quarters in the back of the shop as a type of "fortress—the old iron bed barricaded on three sides by ramparts of boxes of Betty and Nestlé condensed milk, Grace tinned corn and peas" can also be read as a description of prison space.[29] It is no surprise then that for Chang, quitting the grocery trade is portrayed as the acquisition of freedom—an image that is reminiscent of the slave's flight from the plantation.

Through such images, Chinese West Indians reimagine shop space such that it is no longer a place of luxury, power, and privilege as it is so often imagined by authors who remain on the other side of the shop counter. Instead, the shop is redefined as a space of confinement, restriction, and dehumanizing exploitation. Thus, life *beyond* the counter becomes the space of privilege, possibility, and, more importantly in terms of a slave narrative, the space of freedom. Such reenvisioning of shop space is not only radical in its reassignment of positions of privilege; it is also a bold imaginative means by which the Chinese shopkeeper can be depicted as one of the oppressed. In this way, the narratives of oppression and exploitation that have become so important in performing West Indian nationhood are made applicable to the Chinese communities. As such, these images of shop space provide the Chinese with a potent means of claiming belonging within the West Indies.

A New Creole Melody

Chinese West Indians also rewrite the West Indian creole narrative to explicitly include Chineseness. In many of Lee's poems, for example, the Chinese narrative voices are not only unapologetic in their pride in their Chinese heritage, but they are also confident of its value in West Indian space. The reimagining of Jamaican rural space as expansive enough to include Chinese ethnicity is perhaps most evident in a series of poems that detail the intimate life of a Chinese shopkeeper and his Black creole Jamaican wife. "Language Class," for example, relates how the wife tries to teach her husband to speak English and in the process learns how to speak Chinese.[30] The experience portrayed in the poem provides a radical reenvisioning of Jamaican space when the wife learns to speak "his strange language/ as though she were born in it."[31] The wife has, in a sense, become Sinocized, and in so doing, "Jamaican space" is also metaphorically transformed. That which has been deemed "strange" or out of place, in this case, speaking Chinese, becomes "native"—the wife speaks Chinese as if she "were born in it." Similarly, "Birthday Song" and "One World" literally insert a Chinese voice into Jamaican space. In "Birthday Song," although the child is being born in Jamaica, he enters the world to the sound of ancient Chinese melodies. Significantly, the Chinese song is not depicted as being a discordant note in the Jamaican village. This is evident in the mother's reaction to the song: "though the words were strange/ her full heart/ beat to the rhythm of his voice/ and matched his tune/ with the melody of her own fulfilment."[32] Rather than being in conflict with the "melody of Jamaica," the Chinese music finds a matching rhythm and melody in the mother. Jamaican and Chinese spaces are therefore represented as being in harmony with each other. In a similar fashion, "One World" uses music to portray the coming together of Chinese and Jamaican cultural elements to create new and unique music specific to the Jamaican context: the Chinese husband and his Black wife are described as "singing ancient unfamiliar songs of each other's world/ trying to get the words right/ and the tune right."[33] Again, it is the fact that the music of both "worlds" are present in Jamaican space, not clashing inharmoniously but working together to create a new song that expresses the acceptance of Chineseness within the Jamaican landscape. Indeed, the musical imagery has particular resonance, as there is a well-established tradition of representing Jamaican cultural space as a place where "the melody of Europe and the rhythm of Africa" came together to create a new music.[34] Lee's poetry expands on this long-standing image and asserts the validity of Chinese belonging in this space by unabashedly adding the music of China to the mix. Thus, Lee transforms the meaning of Chineseness such that it no longer represents alien or outsider; rather, it is just another way of "being Jamaican."

Beyond Bloodlines

Placing the Chinese overtly within the West Indian narrative of struggle or locating Chineseness in the Jamaican landscape are ways in which Chinese West Indian authors "claim West Indianness." I use the word "claim" self-consciously as a means of reinvoking foundational scholarship on Asian American literature that noted an important theme of "claiming America." In response to such fiction, Elaine Kim asked if

> [s]o much writing by Asian Americans is focused on the theme of claiming an American, as opposed to Asian, identity that we may begin to wonder if this constitutes accommodation, a collective colonized spirit—the fervent wish to "hide our ancestry," which is impossible for us anyway, to relinquish our marginality, and to lose ourselves in an intense identification with the hegemonic culture.[35]

A similar attempt to "lose oneself" within the boundaries of West Indian identity by rendering ethnic difference invisible is also evident in the work of Chinese West Indians. For example, Chen grounds his assertion that he is "*really* a Trinidadian" on the fact that he grew up among Blacks and Indians and feels that he is particularly familiar with their troubles.[36] In a similar fashion, Chang asserts that he and his siblings are more Jamaican than his parents or his brother who was raised in China, because their lifestyles—what they eat and how they speak, for example—were more heavily influenced by their Black Jamaican nursemaid. In addition, Chang specifically points to his loss of the Hakka language during his teenage years as evidence of his "Jamaicanization."

Such comments are a means of portraying the Chinese—Chang and his siblings and Chen—as belonging in the West Indies; however, ironically they also imply an understanding of West Indian space that excludes Chineseness. To "be seen" as West Indian means to "be not seen" as Chinese, and to choose to participate in those cultural signifiers that are particularly associated with an Afro-Euro creole West Indian culture. Thus, in such articulations of national belonging, Chineseness remains uncommon in the common culture. In reality, they reveal boundaries set in an ethnic-based concept of the nation in both the narrative of shared struggle and of creolization, even if in the latter case the narrative appears, at least on a superficial level, to be grounded in broader civic-based ideas of nationhood.

Such representations of nationhood suggest that Chinese West Indians ironically repeat "what they seek to overthrow"—that is, a limited concept of nation enclosed in ethnic boundaries, "[O]ld ideologies [are] being reinforced over and over again." Because of this, the images by Chinese West Indians examined so far can be thought of as what theorist Rey Chow might describe as a "*strategic* attitude" to inscribe Chinese belonging in the West Indies.[37] Chow's definition of strategic approaches to identity formation emerges as part of her attempt to find ways to construct and maintain oppositional discourses that resist hegemonic, essentialist discourses of ethnic identities, in this case, an essentialized Chineseness, in the context of diasporic studies. Her comments have relevance, however, for thinking through ways in which one might also challenge the discourses of identity as expressed in national narratives. Chow suggests that the failure of the strategic approach to challenge discursive borders of ethnic identities is that at its core, it ultimately reasserts the concept of ethnicity and ethnic difference. Thus, Chow argues that those who use this approach are committed to providing "oneself with one's own place" among other ethnic identifications.[38] In other words, by participating in such strategies, one reveals a commitment "to the building, growth and fortification of this [field of ethnicities]."[39] In an analogous fashion, representations of Chinese inclusion in the nation that are based on rendering Chineseness invisible so as to be included in an ethnicized narrative of nation create "new 'solidarities' whose ideological premises remain unquestioned," namely, an underlying belief in the legitimacy of the ethnic-based construction of nation.[40]

For Chow, it is more radical to take a "tactical approach" to representing the nation. Such an approach is "a calculated action determined by the absence of a proper locus"; in other words, one that is not, committed to "the field."[41] In this case, such an approach would include ignoring ethnicity as a means of rejecting the "submission to consanguinity" that is understood to define Chineseness as expressed in national narratives.[42] It is this type of tactical intervention that disrupts the significance of Chineseness for the construction of identity that one finds in the depiction of the Chinese in the fiction of Meiling Jin and Janice Lowe Shinebourne. In Jin's short story "Victoria" and Shinebourne's two novels, *Timepiece* and *The Last English Plantation*, both authors reject creating a "new solidarity" with ideologies that reaffirm the significance of a nationness or Chineseness defined by bloodline and ethnocultural markers. As Ien Ang might put it, their work interrogates "the very significance of the category of Chineseness [and nation] per se as a predominant marker of identification and distinction."[43] Indeed, their depictions of Guyana entirely remove the nation from a "proper locus" in ethnic identification by grounding the boundaries of belonging solely in shared experiences, values, and ambitions.

Ethnic prioritization in the nation therefore becomes irrelevant as does the question of whether or not Chineseness belongs within the nation.

Although these pieces of fiction are set in very different time periods, both Shinebourne and Jin have a similar vision of Guyana as a nation that once consisted of two nonethnically specific spaces of belonging: urban and rural spaces. Similarly, both authors set their stories in times of transition in which a growing ascendancy of political power for urban spaces is depicted as eventually disrupting and destroying the intercultural communal ways of living that had developed in rural areas. These stories provide an important vision not only of the disintegration of rural communities but also of the boundaries within which Guyanese nationhood was constructed in relation to ethnicity prior to the mid-twentieth century. Specifically, Shinebourne and, to a lesser extent, Jin suggest that at one time, community belonging and a cultural identity were created on the grounds of a shared history, shared daily experiences, and shared philosophies about life (particularly political ideas) rather than ethnicity. In so doing, these authors reveal ways in which the Chinese can be imagined as valid members of their West Indian nations rather than as aliens and outsiders despite their Chineseness.

For both authors, shared historical experiences become an important measure of belonging. Indeed, one of the themes running through both of Shinebourne's novels is that without knowledge and appreciation of history there can be no real sense of community. In *Timepiece*, for example, the divisive and competitive quality of life in Georgetown is, in Sandra's opinion, very much related to the lack of a sense of continuity with the past. As Sandra herself puts it, "People live as if they have no past."[44] Indeed, the Georgetown residents are depicted as lacking any real understanding of how they came together as a people or of having built a community through shared historical experience. As a result, Georgetown is described as a place of conflict, division, and competition, characterized by a rampant individualism that stands in direct contrast to the communal experiences of Sandra's home village, described as a place where "you could not forget the past, could not escape from it"; "So close was the past here, it was as if the landscape wore many masks and the spirits of the past still lived here."[45] Because of their awareness of their own history—their nearness to their past—the villagers are depicted as having a much more concrete sense of belonging not only to the place where they live but also to each other, as evidenced by the community spirit that runs through the text. It is this awareness of a shared history, specifically a shared struggle against the exploitive powers of colonialism, that creates a unity among the villagers that largely supersedes and ignores ethnic difference.

The important role given to the knowledge of shared historical experience in creating a sense of belonging is also evident in *The Last English Plantation*. Indeed, in this novel the link between a connection to one's past and one's ability to situate oneself in the present is made even more explicit in the way in which Nani reacts to June's first day of school. Nani believes that June's distress over school is attributable to the fact that Lucille did not say a mantra before June began school. Nani tries to rectify the situation by performing the mantra herself—which turns out to be a retelling of family history. The displacement that June feels in the new urbanized school setting is therefore countered by the story of her ancestors' lives in Guyana. Nani literally inserts June within Guyana's long labor history, suggesting that June's sense of belonging should be based on her awareness of her ancestors' experience with colonialism as indentured laborers and the contribution their labor made to the development of the country.

In "Victoria," Jin also recognizes the importance of a common historical past, particularly in terms of the experience of colonialism, as a means of establishing Chinese belonging in Guyana. "Victoria" begins with the question, "What was a nice Chiney girl doing with a name like Victoria?" The response is asserted in the subsequent line: "It was still the days of Empire, that's why. They call she Victoria in honour of that fat English

Queen that once ruled the waves."[46] The story's imaginative space is thereby established within the colonial time period; and by branding the name of one of the most famous representatives of British colonialism on her Chinese heroine, Jin situates Chinese West Indian experience within the greater colonial West Indian experience. Indeed, with this detail, Jin asserts that the Chinese have been as subjected and oppressed by empire as any other ethnic group in the West Indies.

Jin also establishes belonging for her Chinese characters in this story by focusing on their family's indentured labor history. If West Indian belonging finds its roots in the suffering on the plantation, the claim to share in that history is an important means of appropriating space for the Chinese in the West Indies. It is the same device that Shinebourne uses in *The Last English Plantation* when Cyrus responds to Boysie's suggestions that Cyrus' loyalties are not with the villagers. Cyrus defends himself by recounting his father's experiences as an estate laborer. Essentially, Shinebourne makes a link between Cyrus' ability to place himself within the community and his father's history of suffering on the plantations. Jin is even more effective in embedding her Chinese characters within the suffering that colonialism created in Guyana when she describes the casual brutality enacted against Victoria's grandfather and fellow Chinese immigrants. Jin writes, "That is why you get the saying, a Chinee is a Chinee, just shoot any damn goobi."[47] The semantic structure of the sentence allows Jin to depict Chinese belonging as a fait accompli through idiom: the Chinese become embedded in the very language of Guyana while at the same time, the historical justification for this inclusion, their suffering under colonialism, is also established.

History is not, however, the only way to claim belonging for Chinese characters. For Chinese West Indian authors, belonging finds its truest expression in everyday shared experiences, most importantly, in a common struggle for survival. For both Jin and Shinebourne, the rural Chinese shop is imagined as a key component in the struggle for existence for all West Indians. Shop life and village life are depicted as being intrinsically intertwined, such that shop space is no longer represented as alien space. Neither Wong nor Ben treats his shop as a profit-motivated enterprise. Instead, both men see their shops as being a means by which all of the villagers struggle to live. Thus, they are willing to continue to extend credit to the villagers even when it is obvious that these bills cannot be paid, for their focus is not on what they can take from the villagers but on what they can contribute to their communities. Wong expresses this attitude succinctly in response to Victoria's complaints that they can no longer afford to give credit: "A man got to feed his family."[48] Thus Wong and Ben are represented as being on the "side" of the villagers, not as outsiders who are removed from their struggles but as participants in the very same struggle. Their integration into the community is most vividly demonstrated in the fact that both Wong's and Ben's shops fail specifically because the shops are so tied up with the lives of the villagers.

The failures of the Chinese shops in "Victoria" and *Timepiece* not only suggest that their Chinese owners are intrinsically involved in the lives of their communities; they also provide an opportunity to radically re-represent Chinese shop space. With such business failures, the Chinese shop is no longer depicted simply as "Chinese space"; rather, it becomes firmly identified as "village space." A brief but powerful statement by Jin provides one of the best images of the coterminous existence of shop space and village space. In describing the villagers' reaction to a pay cut, Jin writes, "There was one big grumbling on the estate, you had only fo stand in the shop to hear it."[49] From a very literal standpoint, such a statement means simply that the same complaints made on the estate are also made in the shop; but the structure of the phrase suggests a more figurative interpretation, which, in turn, provides a striking example of the interconnectedness of shop and village space. If one needs only stand in the shop to hear the grumbling on the estate, then, in a sense, the estate and the shop are the same space. "Chinese space," that is, the shop space, and "West Indian space," that is, plantation space, are thereby collapsed into one. In this sense, Chinese space *is* West Indian space.

Shared daily experience as the measure by which characters can claim belonging in the West Indies regardless of ethnicity is also an important theme in *The Last English Plantation.* For example, early in the novel June recalls life in Old Dam. It is an existence in which ethnicity was of less importance than shared experiences in the establishment of the community's boundaries of belonging.

> Half of the families in Old Dam had been African, living in cottages set a little way from the logies where Indian families lived. Yet *they had lived like one large family in spite of their differences*, the women sharing childminding and attending each other's birth, marriage and funeral rituals. They all, men and women, used to gossip and talk work and politics. She missed the feeling of belonging to that kind of village. (Emphasis added.)[50]

> [It was] the closeness of people with the same struggles, trials and tribulations who did not just talk about them and listen sympathetically but did things together all the time—helping each other give birth, mind the old, bury the dead, care for the sick and contain the criminal elements.[51]

In New Dam, however, Lucille rejects the communal culture that is based on shared rural experience because it is tainted by the poverty and social marginalization that she is trying so hard to escape. As a result, Lucille constantly distances herself and her family from her neighbors and their daily experiences: she insists on speaking English with an imitation British accent and refuses (or cannot) speak Hindi; she no longer spends Sundays cooking meals with the other village women; and, she sends June to high school in the city—an accomplishment that no other family from their immediate community seems to have the resources to do. Lucille even insists that Cyrus move the new toilet he is building farther away from the road to ensure that people in the community will be less inclined to share in its use. In the end, because she distances herself from the shared daily rituals and events of the community, Lucille ends up essentially isolated, alienated from her husband, daughter, and neighbors. The most extreme example of her alienation is perhaps the moment at Mariam's funeral when June realizes how Lucille is "aloof from it. . . . She was only here for manner's sake."[52] The significance of this moment for this discussion lies in the fact that it reveals that for Lucille neither belonging nor alienation is predicated on her ethnicity; rather, belonging is based simply on shared daily experiences.

It is the same lack of common, everyday experience that eventually separates June and Sandra from their childhood village friends. As students in an urban high school, their daily lives differ vastly from that of their mutual classmate Ralph Brijall, for example, who has left school to work on the estate. In both novels, Chineseness as a means of marking out spaces of belonging for both girls is irrelevant. How they live their lives becomes the deciding factor in determining whether or where they belong. To this end, it is interesting to note that on beginning high school, June does not make any attempt to become friends with any of the other Chinese students. Despite a shared ethnic background, June clearly feels no connection to them. Significantly, the distance that June feels from them has to do with the space to which the Chinese students are understood to belong. They are clearly city people—they "looked at home" in the city—while June feels alienated in urban space.[53] June therefore initially seeks to find a place for herself at the school by associating with the rural children. Indeed, the validity of her claim to belong in rural space is demonstrated when the city children call her "Country Bacoo."[54]

Jin's story "Short Fuse" provides yet another example of the integration of Chinese characters into West Indian space on the basis of shared experience, although this time, "West Indian space" is not so much the literal territory of Guyana as it is the emotional milieu of a West Indian migrant to England.

The sense of exile and alienation that Gladys feels as a result of the hostility directed toward her in her new British environment has nothing to do with her being of Chinese ancestry. It does, however, have everything to do with her being an immigrant. In fact, Gladys' experiences of displacement are representative of those of any West Indian migrant to England regardless of his or her specific ethnic background: "From the first week in Inverness Terrace, when the landlady lifted the lids of her cooking pot to peer inside, Gladys was aware of hostility. She knew the look that said, no coloreds, no children, no animals, and bore each insult, each act of hostility as a mark of her exile."[55] In fact, so invisible is Gladys' Chineseness in this exploration of West Indian immigration that if she did not eventually identify herself as being of Chinese ancestry there would be no way for the reader to know her ethnic heritage. Gladys eats and talks like any other Guyanese migrant; similarly, when homesick, she dreams of Guyana, not of China. For Gladys, being a West Indian immigrant to England means that she occupies that space designated for all West Indians in England—"colored space"—regardless of her Chinese background. Seen simply as just another West Indian by those around her, Gladys' claim to West Indian identity is validated.

In *Timepiece*, the characters divide themselves into gendered spaces defined by their experiences and the expectations placed on them as men and women in Guyana rather than by ethnicity. This division into what can be described as "communities of gender" is yet another means of downplaying the significance of ethnicity in establishing belonging. It is most explicitly explored in the depiction of Ben and Helen's relationships with each other and with their friends.

Both Ben and Helen are members of a tight circle of friends of their own gender, "each group close, loyal and indivisible."[56] Of Ben and his friends, Shinebourne writes, "[T]heir conversations were a reaffirmation of *belonging to each other and their places of work and male authority*" (emphasis added).[57] Sandra's male colleagues are described in much the same way, in spite of their different political and economic positions, that is, as being immersed in "the rudeness of being Guianese men together, the wrongness and the strongness of it all."[58] As with Nunez's *Bruised Hibiscus,* the men in *Timepiece* find their identity—that is, their place of belonging—in their shared belief that women are inferior beings whom they have the right to dominate, control, and even abuse. Thus, it is that arguments with Helen routinely degenerate into Ben's reminder that Helen "keep *her place;* her job was to keep the children fed and house clean, clothes washed and food cooked" (emphasis added).[59] Essentially, Ben's attitude affirms the understanding that in Guyana there is a sociocultural place for men and a place for women based on gendered identities that subsume ethnic difference.

Sandra experiences similar treatment from the men in her life. For example, no man ever wants to allow her the last word in an argument or debate. Additionally, as a female reporter, not only is she expected to cover less politically focused events, such as beauty contests, she is literally placed in "female space," when she is assigned a desk that is explicitly labeled "female reporter." In fact, when Sandra writes and submits a thoughtful, critical political piece to her editor, she is accused of plagiarism because her editor does not believe that something of that quality could be written by a woman. Eventually, Sandra describes her experiences as the "cross of her womanhood"—the burden of being treated as a second-class citizen simply because one is born female.[60] As Lucille puts it in one of the most memorable scenes in *The Last English Plantation*, being a woman in Guyana means one must "carry all the burdens for the men, the burden of the sick, the old, the children, burying the dead, and get no thanks for it, only licks!"[61]

The response of Helen and her friends to the reality of being born a woman in a fiercely patriarchal society is to draw together and to create an alternative space, free from the bonds of "that cross." It is the knowledge that they all share the same denigrating experiences as women—not as specifically Black women or Chinese women or Indian women—that allows them to come together: "The women's talk too was a form of binding, but also a release from their confinement not only as plantation people, but also as women at home."[62] Their bond is the burden of womanhood, not ethnicity and their desire to be free from the burdens inherent in the labels "wife," "mother," "daughter," "sister," and "woman."

The gap between Helen and Ben in *Timepiece* is not simply a gender divide; they also represent very different philosophical positions or responses to the unsettled times in which they live, just as in *The Last English Plantation*, Lucille, Boysie, and Cyrus each symbolically represent different responses to the anxieties of pre-independence Guyana. What these characters are disputing is essentially, "the ways of doing things, of living"; "Beneath their everyday lives this struggle of ideas went on constantly."[63] The choice of how to live on a sociopolitical level is also represented as an important means of establishing belonging for the Chinese of the West Indies that renders ethnic difference irrelevant.

For Jin and Shinebourne, the pursuit of middle-class respectability defined in British standards of norms, styles, and values is one of the potential "ways of living" in which their Chinese characters, specifically the women, can define spaces of belonging for themselves. For example, Esther is memorably described as a "converted Christian and a converted 'lady' besides."[64] As such, she tries her best to assimilate herself and her family to what she believes are the standards of urban respectability: she wants her father-in-law to wear store-bought clothing; she hopes that Victoria will lose her "Berbice talk"; and is delighted when Victoria makes friends with Nettie Lee, "a Georgetown girl [who] had been to the Ursuline Convent School in Church Street."[65] Esther keeps her modern-styled city home immaculate, insists on saying grace before meals, and to Wong's discomfort, serves food like sandwiches rather than roti. Her identity is drawn from her community of church friends who share similar goals and lifestyle ambitions. They express no concerns about any differences in ethnicity since they are so busy "being British." Shinebourne is perhaps most explicit in capturing how the desire to assimilate to British standards can subsume other ethnic differences in *The Last English Plantation* when Lucille asserts: "This is the West Indies, not India, not Africa, not China, the West Indies! We are British."[66] In the opinion of women like Esther, Lucille, and to a lesser extent, Helen, West Indian identity is defined as "being British" and is available to members of any ethnic group as long as they are willing to assimilate to British cultural standards and norms. In their minds, membership in the nation is available to all who are willing to "be British."

Shared political affiliation or interests is yet another "way of living" in which Chinese West Indian authors assert belonging for their Chinese characters without having to refer to ethnicity. This depiction of a group identity in which ethnicity plays a minimal role runs particularly strong in Shinebourne's fiction, perhaps because Shinebourne lived in Guyana in the mid-twentieth century and is acutely aware of the terrible consequences of aligning political differences with ethnic and racial division. In fact, in *Timepiece*, Shinebourne writes: "If you lived by race in this country it killed you one way or the other—you either stifled in your own narrow inwardness or you engaged in conflict. There had to be another way."[67] To a large degree, both of Shinebourne's novels can be read as the attempt to find (or return to) this "other way of being" politically speaking—to imagine Guyana as a space where race or ethnicity is not inherently connected to political communities or used to create violent divisions between ethnic groups in the pursuit of politics. Indeed, *The Last English Plantation* and *Timepiece* both work hard to depict Guyana as a place where ethnic conflict is revealed to actually mask a split between rural and urban interests that has been manipulated by politicians into ethnic division and animosity. In *Timepiece*, for example, Paul claims that the race riots are "all politics man. . . . Those damn politicians as usual. . . . They stir up and ferment the people, but no-one blames them for it publicly. They just say Guiana has race problems. Is politician problem we have."[68]

To further reinforce her idea that, at and around the time of independence, ethnic division became a lazy and dangerous way of expressing political division, Shinebourne's novels depict a Guyana in which ethnic division is deemed to be an unnatural political development. The parallel experiences of Sandra and Son's childhoods are particularly significant in this regard. Sandra notes, for example, that growing up in the country, "my race didn't seem to matter to anyone," while Son, who grew up in the city, had a similar experience: "It didn't use to be an issue what race you are except when it was a gibe and it hurt, and your mother and father, if you lucky to have one, would soothe it like so with a kiss."[69] In *The Last English Plantation*, the unnatural connection between politics and ethnicity is also revealed in Cyrus' response when Boysie complains that June should not play with the White overseer's daughter. Instead of framing the division between overseer and estate laborer in terms of ethnicity in the way that Boysie does, Cyrus comments, "I t'ink he was really talking politics. You know how people always mix up the two."[70]

If political differences along ethnic lines are not "natural," how is it that ethnicity and politics become so easily entangled? Shinebourne also addresses this question in her work, particularly in *The Last English Plantation*. In this novel, she reveals that the association between politics and ethnicity is largely enacted through processes of representation in which rural interests and rural space become designated as "Indo-Guyanese space," and urban interests and spaces are represented as "Afro-Guyanese space." In one of *The Last English Plantation*'s most memorable scenes, Lucille accuses June of wanting to be a "coolie woman" because of June's stubborn retention of her community ties despite the fact that she is now a student in the city. For the most part, in her long rant against her daughter, Lucille uses the term "coolie" as a synonym for "rural poor"; however, "being coolie" is also represented as being more specifically bound to Indo-Guyanese experiences such that the more Lucille talks, the more "coolie" begins to represent "Indo-Guyanese" as much as it represents "rural poor." Thus, for Lucille, "being coolie" is explicitly associated with marrying Indo-Guyanese men, speaking Hindi, learning mantras, and doing puja, all of which are activities and ways of life obviously associated with a large proportion of individuals of Indo-Guyanese backgrounds. By representing rural experience in this manner, Lucille defines rural communities and rural life as being Indo-Guyanese.

In a similar fashion, urban space is represented by other characters as being Afro-Guyanese space. For example, Sergeant Richards' argument that Mr. Easen should not be involved in the dispute over Ralph's imprisonment is based on the fact that Richards believes that Easen, as an Afro-Guyanese, is out of place in a rural setting—that he belongs in city space: "Times changing, Easen . . . Black man 'in slave in this country no more. You can continue living like slave with coolie 'pon sugar plantation. You don know black man lef' plantation long time now? You still living in ancient history? Well, road getting build now. You can ride 'pon you bicycle on smooth smooth road all the way to Georgetown now."[71]

In resisting the attraction to ethnic prioritization, Shinebourne's novels also suggest that an ethnic approach to national belonging has significant implications for the representation of Chinese characters within the West Indies, and more specifically, within Guyana. If to belong in Guyana, one must be a member of a limited number of ethnic groups, then it is most likely that the Chinese will be written out of nation space—deemed invalid—unless they are able to submerge their ethnic and cultural differences. In other words, to "be seen" as valid members of the nation, Chineseness must, paradoxically, become invisible. Thus, Sandra complains that "in Georgetown, Indianness as I lived it in Pheasant is alien. . . . Here in Georgetown I'm not treated as a rural Indian. I think I'm seen partly as Chinese."[72] Sandra's difficulty with "being seen as Chinese" rather than as Indian lies in the fact that Sandra has aligned herself with rural issues. She feels at home in rural space; but for Sandra, to "be rural" seems to mean that on some level she believes that she must "be seen" as "Indian." Being seen as Chinese somehow sets her apart from rural space and the identity that she has claimed for herself.

In describing June's experience on the first day of school Shinebourne is even more explicit in suggesting the potential "writing out" of the Chinese unless they are "seen" as members of an alternate ethnic group. The classroom environment quickly degenerates into a power struggle between the city and country children that mirrors the political struggle that is developing on a national scale. When June tries to become involved, Rita, one of the city Indians (significantly, responding to her friend's comment that Rita put June in her "place"), simply "put her fingers to her eyes and pulled them upwards into thin slits, 'Chinky Chinee!'"[73] In doing so, Rita signals that June is outside of the conflict specifically on the basis of her "Chineseness." June does not belong. June seems to recognize that by being seen as Chinese, she is being placed outside of the fracas, for she responds to Rita by announcing, "I am Indian too!"[74] By claiming an Indian identity, June asserts that she is a valid participant in the classroom struggle—a validity that has been challenged because of the visibility of her Chineseness.

Identity beyond Borders

In many ways, the discussion of Chineseness in this chapter can be understood to be implicitly part of a broader, as yet largely unacknowledged, debate over the question, what does it meant to be part of a Chinese diaspora? It is a question that, if acknowledged, poses a challenge to the boundaries of ethnicity itself by pointing to the permeability of ethnocultural boundaries and to the political impetus that often lies behind their construction. An awareness of the flexible nature of ethnicity has long been central to the theorization of diaspora, particularly in cultural studies. There is, in other words, no essential Chinese West Indian identity but rather, as many ways of being Chinese as there are of being West Indian. In this regard, Stuart Hall's argument concerning the construction of British "Blackness" also applies to the construction of Chineseness.

> What is at issue here is the recognition of the extraordinary diversity of subject positions, social experiences and cultural identities which compose the category ["Chinese"]; that is the recognition that ["Chinese"] is essentially a politically and culturally constructed category, which cannot be grounded in a set of fixed transcultural or transcendental racial categories and which therefore has no guarantees in Nature. What this brings into play is the recognition of the immense diversity and differentiation of the historical and cultural experiences of ["Chinese"] subjects.[75]

Chinese West Indian authors' depictions of West Indian Chineseness give substance to Hall's assertion when they explore the heterogeneity within the category "Chinese." In doing so, their work not only draws attention to the constitutive and flexible nature of belonging within West Indian spaces; it also asserts the varied ways of being Chinese and take up Ang's challenge to

> resist the convenient and comforting reduction of Chineseness as a seemingly natural and certain racial essence; . . . to break out of the prisonhouse of Chineseness and embrace lives—personal, social, political—. . . to construct open-ended and plural "post-Chinese" identities through investments in continuing cross-influences of diverse, lateral, unanticipated intercultural encounters in the world at large.[76]

In the process, these authors significantly disrupt the stereotypical polarization between being Chinese and being West Indian that has been so often used to define the boundaries of the nation. They also reify ambiguity as a central component of belonging to any identity instead of identifying it as a problem to be resolved. In other words, they assert that there are many ways of being Chinese.

One of the most obvious ways in which some Chinese West

Indian authors contest homogenized and limited understandings of Chineseness is in their exploration of what it means to be an "eleven o'clock child"—a term apparently used by Jamaican Hakka Chinese to identify individuals of Chinese descent born in Jamaica rather than in China.[77] The very act of differentiating between China-born and West Indian–born Chinese children destabilizes cohesive and homogeneous representations of the Chinese because it forces the reader to recognize difference within that category and raises the question, what does it mean to be an "eleven o'clock child"?

For Chang, this question does not appear to become entirely resolved. For example, his definition of "eleven o'clock children" implies that from the perspective of the China-born Chinese, the eleven o'clock children have a "not quite" Chinese status: "[W]e missed the fullness of noon, of being born in China itself."[78] In fact, Chang, who was born in Jamaica, has lost his ancestral language and has been heavily influenced by Black Jamaican culture; he defines himself as being "more Jamaican than Chinese."[79] In contrast, the identity of Chang's brother, who is born in China, is never in doubt. Separated from the English language and Jamaican creole culture, the brother is clearly identified as Chinese. By focusing on the loss of those cultural traits associated with Chinese ethnicity as the underlying factors that make him "more Jamaican" Chang reestablishes a polarization between being Chinese and being Jamaican that leads him away from the interesting question of whether or not his "more Jamaican" existence can be understood as just another way of being Chinese, rather than as a factor that alienates him from claiming a Chinese identity.

While such attention to the eleven o' clock children is a significant means of revealing that "the Chinese" is not a monolithic community, Chinese West Indian authors rarely attempt to truly explore the implications of this reality in terms of the construction of ethnic and national spaces of belonging. It is in Shinebourne's most recent work, however, that a resistance to limited understandings of ethnicity—that contesting of ethnicity *within* ethnicity itself that Hall asserts—is more fully mounted. Shinebourne's more recent fiction moves away from the historical focus of her earlier works and engages more directly with the question of whether it is "so important to be Chinese or possible to be Chinese here in British Guiana"; that is, "Can One Say No to Chineseness?"[80] This question that lies at the root of some of her newest fiction challenges the stability of cultural and ethnic identities, and has significant implications for ideas of national belonging. Shinebourne's fiction suggests that there is no inherently stable identity, just as there is no inherent division between "Chinese" and "West Indian." Instead, the two blur together such that the many ways of being Chinese are really just many ways of being West Indian.

A superficial reading of "The Berbice Marriage Match" may lead one to believe that Shinebourne has actually reinscribed the oft-used representation of a division between "Chinese space" and "West Indian space" such that to be West Indian, a Chinese individual must suppress evidence of his or her Chinese heritage. After all, Ruth and her sisters consider themselves to be Guyanese instead of Chinese since, like their mother, Enid, they were raised Catholic "without any Chinese customs."[81] Furthermore, Enid has some East Indian parentage and, therefore, considers herself not to be "pure" Chinese. The family is contrasted with the Choys, a family which adheres to more traditional Chinese cultural norms and fashions. For example, Mrs. Choy has difficulty speaking English, wears traditional Chinese-style clothing, and keeps her hair in a bun rather than cut and permed in what Enid calls "English-style."[82] The Choys also serve traditional Chinese foods (that are directly contrasted with the creole Guyanese food that Enid and her daughters indulge in on their trip to the Choys), decorate their home with artifacts from China, and observe traditional forms of Chinese etiquette. Such realities lead Enid to feel that with the Choys, "she was in the presence of what must surely be a *genuine Chinese*" (emphasis added), just as Alexander's siblings reject the Lis on that the ground that they are "not 'real' Chinese . . . they [are] Creole."[83]

Nevertheless, although the Lis have clearly identified themselves as Guyanese and have lost many of the traditional Chinese ethnic markers, for Shinebourne this does not mean that the Lis cannot also be identified as Chinese. In other words, belonging for the Lis, in terms of a claiming a Guyanese identity, does not necessarily mean "ethnic amnesia" on their part; rather, it means that the Lis have developed a different understanding of being Chinese that is not rigidly bound by ethnocultural or even phenotypical markers. Instead, being Chinese becomes a choice.

Shinebourne's radical representation of ethnic belonging as a matter of choice rather than bloodline, or what Chow might refer to as "the myth of consanguinity," is demonstrated in the simple fact that, regardless of her inability to speak Chinese, her mixed-racial ancestry, and her lack of Chinese customs, Enid considers herself to be Chinese.[84] Enid locates herself within a Chinese identity largely by choice—that is, by regularly listening to lectures on Chinese culture and by associating with the Chinese community of Georgetown. Furthermore, the fact that Enid is accepted as Chinese in Georgetown but finds difficulty being accepted as such in the country reinforces the concept that ethnicity changes per location in time and space. Thus Shinebourne undermines the most stable boundaries of "Chinese space" in the West Indies—physical features—in dramatic fashion. In other words, if Chineseness is a matter of choice, "looking Chinese" does not mean that one must necessarily claim a Chinese identity. One can choose otherwise. In a sense, Shinebourne had suggested such an idea earlier in her writing when, in *Timepiece*, Sandra chooses to "be Indian" despite her obvious Chinese ancestry.[85] In an even more explicit way, in "The Berbice Marriage Match," Enid's daughters reject the concept that their features and ancestry constrain them to being Chinese, whatever that might be, when they make the seemingly unproblematic decision that they will just be Guyanese.

Shinebourne's depiction of Enid and her daughters also suggests another radical understanding of ethnicity that challenges the boundaries of belonging: namely, her writing suggests that distinct ethnic identities exist only when there is some benefit to be gained from them. It is the same concept that Hall explores when, writing about Black British identity, he argues:

> "[B]lack" was coined as a way of referencing the common experience of racism and marginalization in Britain and came to provide the organizing category of a new politics of resistance, amongst groups and communities with, in fact, very different histories, traditions and ethnic identities. In this moment, politically speaking, "The Black experience," as a singular and unifying framework . . . became "hegemonic."[86]

In "The Berbice Marriage Match" Chineseness does not have political value, but it can bring about financial gain.[87] After all, by choosing to place herself within Chinese space in Guyana, Enid is able to access the financial assistance of the Chinese community in the raising of her family. Similarly, Ruth's ability to be seen as Chinese will ensure a marriage with a financially stable man. In fact, Ruth's surprise decision to go through with the arranged marriage is partially based on her recognition that such a union would bring about some very specific material benefits for her and her family.

> Canje was not a bad place. It was big and spacious. It was a good place to raise a family. It was somewhere her sisters and mother could visit to get away from Georgetown. . . . [P]erhaps Alexander would do so well they would live in their own house and she would be able to look after her mother in her old age. . . . His bakery was also doing well. He was a breadwinner. . . . He could be the best husband she would get.[88]

"The Berbice Marriage Match" is also radical in its suggestion that West Indian space actually facilitates Chineseness rather than being antagonistic to its presence. In comparison, in "Light in the Shop" West Indian Jamaican space erodes Chineseness, and in *Mr. On Loong*, Chinese and West Indian spaces are mutually exclusive. For Shinebourne, however, West Indian space is the condition under which a myriad equally valid ways of being Chinese can occur. This is symbolized by the matchmaker's role, played by the schoolteacher Elizabeth Waldron. Significantly, although her name identifies her as being a Creole West Indian, it is Elizabeth who acts as a translator between the two families, in both practical terms (she conducts correspondence on behalf of Mrs. Choy) and in more metaphorical terms (she explains the history of the Chinese in Guyana to the Li sisters). Elizabeth's role is essentially that of a negotiator between different understandings and expressions of Chineseness: Enid's and her daughters' less ethnically restrictive living out of Chineseness and the Choys' more traditionally marked out Chinese identity. To a large degree, it is because Elizabeth plays this facilitating role that Ruth and Alexander, two very different examples of being Chinese, are able to come together with the potential of having children and continuing to create alternative ways of being Chinese.

Despite such seeming flexibility, however, Shinebourne's Chinese characters show an awareness of the fact that their physical features do impact their ability to construct and perform their identities; or, as Ien Ang recognized, "[w]hile scientific racism has long been discarded . . . the notion of race continues to thrive in everyday life, where race theories operate in practice as popular epistemologies of ethnic distinction, discrimination, and identification."[89] Shinebourne addresses the salience of race and its impact on the negotiation of identity in the short story "London and New York" by focusing on the false boundaries that physical features can establish in terms of determining where one belongs. It is an argument that, by extension, has the possibility of further destabilizing national boundaries that are situated within ideas of ethnicized belonging. In other words, in this story, Shinebourne undermines the "immediacy of recognition" and its relationship to identities that Fanon discussed in his exploration of "Blackness" by creating a character who continually transcends boundaries of ethnic and cultural belonging that are closely related to her phenotypical features. Simply put, Shinebourne explicitly rejects as artificial the limitations that physical features can place on one's ability to belong. This challenge is symbolically posited early in the story when the narrator remembers how her father had placed dividers in his shop so that there would be separate spaces for male and female customers. Shinebourne draws attention to the fact that these dividers were artificial and that in reality, both men and women were contained in the one shop space. Further, Shinebourne goes on to celebrate the removal of such artificial spaces of belonging when she writes: "[I]n Father's place, it was the times that the barriers between these came down that he liked, the times you would find men and women, children and adults not in an exclusive space, but talking to each other."[90]

The challenge that Shinebourne poses to the artificial exclusionary boundaries of ethnic identities in "London and New York" is developed through the narrator's experience in three restaurants in and around London. Each restaurant represents three spaces of belonging in terms of identity for the narrator: a Chinese restaurant, an Indian restaurant, and a restaurant serving traditional Afro-Creole Guyanese food. Each of these spaces is a "home space" for the narrator, despite the fact that they seem to be such distinctly separated spaces and that she does not "look" quite right in any of them: at the Chinese restaurant, the food reminds the narrator of her Indian grandmother's cooking; the Indian restaurant's curries are deemed to be somewhat similar to the Guyanese curries that make up "part of the creole diet"; and the menu at the Afro-Guyanese restaurant reflects that of her mother's and her own cooking.[91] Importantly, even though all three restaurants are specifically associated with different ethnic identities, they are also sites of boundary transgression that destroy the very borders that they assert. Thus, at the Chinese restaurant, the narrator declares, "I taste East Indian duck in their Chinese duck, I taste Guyanese callaloo in Chinese greens."[92] Similarly, the Indian restaurant is not only filled with people from different ethnic groups, a reality that reveals that it is not exclusively "Indian space," the curry prepared there is different from what she eats at home and in Guyana, even though the dishes are both identified as curry. There are, in other words, alternate ways of "cooking Indian" just as there are alternate ways of "being Indian." Thus, the restaurants symbolize the reality that there are no absolute boundaries in terms of the narrator's space of belonging. It is this reality that is further developed when the narrator travels to Chinatown, New York.

In Chinatown, despite its clear designation as a "Chinese space" that corresponds with the narrator's physical features, the narrator feels "lost, far away from home."[93] She is particularly struck by the vast differences between "Chinese space" in London and "Chinese space" in New York, a difference that once again draws attention to the fact that Chineseness is experienced differently depending on one's location. This part of the story centers on the narrator's search for red bean cakes, a food that is traditionally associated with the Chinese New Year. The narrator is unable to find the red bean cakes that she was familiar with as a child in Guyana in New York's Chinatown, although in England, she would normally find them in London's traditional Chinese district. In the end, the narrator only locates the bean cakes that she is familiar with when she leaves "Chinese space" and enters "Guyanese space," namely, a Guyanese restaurant in the traditionally understood "Black space" of Brooklyn. The narrator concludes that the bean cakes "had become a metaphor of home" and, further, that the definition of "home" (a space of belonging) is clearly neither stable nor absolute.[94] Thus, the story reveals the artificiality of a static understanding of identity that is at the heart of concepts such as belonging or national boundaries. Instead, "home" or "belonging" are revealed to be constantly redefined, negotiated, disturbed, and lived in a variety of ways: "In London I get red bean cakes in Chinatown but not in Guyanese restaurants. In New York I do not find them in Chinatown but in a Guyanese restaurant in Brooklyn. As I ate the cake, I felt I had arrived in New York but the journey I took to get here was one in which I had to negotiate a chain of cultural translations to get 'home.'"[95]

This idea of cultural translations and negotiation is important to understanding Shinebourne's radical reenvisioning of what it means to be Chinese or to belong in the West Indies. Her point is that identity is constantly being reworked and transformed, an idea that has particularly inclusive ramifications for the understanding of where the Chinese belong within the imaginative boundaries of West Indian communities. It is, according to Shinebourne's vision, impossible to contain Chineseness within rigid, codified spaces. As with other ethnic identities within the West Indies, Chineseness must be understood as an open category that contains many ways of being; furthermore, any West Indian identity, including national identity, is in constant flux. This sense of flux and openness that defines what it means to be West Indian and to belong in the West Indies is highlighted by Shinebourne in a scene in which the narrator speaks to a woman from the Dominican Republic. Unlike other characters whom the narrator has encountered, this Caribbean woman quickly identifies the fact that the narrator has both an English and a Caribbean accent. Importantly, she does not seem to find the two accents at odds with each other or with the narrator's physical features. Instead, the woman simply accepts them as part of the narrator's reality as a West Indian woman. This encounter leads the narrator to make one of Shinebourne's most definitive statements on West Indian identity in terms of belonging in West Indian space when the narrator comments "Caribbean people have developed the skills of cultural translation . . . learning to recognise and use them to map our everyday transactions."[96] In the casual acceptance of the cultural and ethnic boundary transgressions made by the woman and the narrator, West Indian space receives its only definitive boundary: no stable boundaries at all. Rather, it is a space of change and transformation where cultural translation is an "everyday transaction." As such, the concepts of "Chinese," "nation," and even "belonging" are deemed to be both inherently ambiguous and "irretrievably heterogenous."

The self-representation of Chinese West Indians seeks new ways to expand and explore the performance of Chineseness in the context of nation. By expanding on the motif of alienation, challenging limited notions of creolization, and exploring the possibilities and limitations of diaspora, such work insists on the myriad ways of "being Chinese." Such literature also re-envisions West Indian national spaces by providing important challenges to any definition of "West Indian" or "nation" that relies on static and exclusive boundaries. Their work draws attention to the constitutive reality of identities such as "Chinese" by creating images of the Chinese that transgress the boundaries traditionally established for them. By drawing attention to the dynamic, unstable, and inherently heterogeneous nature of categories such as "belonging" and "the Chinese," these Chinese West Indian representations force us to acknowledge the constructed nature of nationhood and the inherent unevenness of belonging within such a space. In so doing, they also bring us closer to looking for, and engaging with, new strategies of representation in which ambiguity as enshrined in multiple national narratives is recognized as the central component of belonging to nation space.

Conclusion

In my parents' home there is a sepia-colored water-damaged photograph that was taken in Kingston, Jamaica, in 1936. It is a formal photograph. In the center sits a brown-skinned woman, her hands resting loosely on the armrests of the chair on which she is seated. To her left stands a three-year-old boy, lower lip starting to protrude as he looks uncertainly at the photographer. To her right, an older boy leans toward the woman over the chair's armrest, staring boldly into the camera. The boys are dressed neatly in the colonial fashion of the day: short pants, long knee socks, and shiny black shoes. Their thick, wavy, dark hair has been neatly parted and combed back to reveal Chinese features. The photograph is of my grandmother, my father, and his older brother. It was taken just before my uncle was sent from Jamaica to be raised by my grandfather's family in China. My uncle was five years old at the time. He would not see his mother, brother, or other siblings again until his return to Jamaica twenty-five years later.

In my mind, my uncle was always something of a mystery. He definitely looked like my father and his sisters, but while to me they were clearly Jamaican, my uncle was something less definitive: he spoke Hakka-accented Jamaican patois; he cooked tofu from scratch, and kept live fish in a big cauldron on the kitchen floor that he would kill right before he cooked them; he wrote notes to himself in Chinese calligraphy; and when his children eventually migrated from China to join him in the United States, the three of them would converse in a language no one else could understand. How exactly did he fit into our family? Where did he belong?

In many ways, the questions that I asked regarding the relationship between my "Chinese uncle" and the rest of our family inspired the questions this research is centered on: What relationships do Chinese West Indians have with other West Indians? How are they perceived? How are they represented in popular discourse? Simply, how do they fit into the nation? Where do they belong?

As a means of answering these questions, I have focused on the different ways in which Chineseness—so often reduced to the stereotype of Mr. Chin—has been represented in West Indian literary texts. In doing so, I also aimed to gain a better understanding of the construction, dissemination, and maintenance of national identities and to challenge a certain marginalization of the cultural contributions of the Chinese in the West Indies. Although there has been some research on the economic role of Chinese West Indians and a growing body of work recording their history, interrogations into the cultural impact of their presence have generally been overlooked. By connecting the long-term literary depictions of the Chinese to overarching narratives of nation, I have attempted to show that literary images of the Chinese have played a seminal role in the production and performance of West Indian cultural identities in colonial and national discourses. Indeed, by reading the literary representations of Chinese interactions with other West Indians as ritualized encounters or symbolic gestures, I also sought to draw attention to the diverse narratives involved in the performance of national identity and account for the multiple locations in which the boundaries of nation have been established. As such, my underlying claim is that the representations of the Chinese found in literary and other texts provide us with a significant position from which to explore the ambiguities, potentialities, and limitations of nation as an imagined construct in the West Indies. Further, these images reveal that neither "nation" nor "belonging" is a stable position. Instead they signify continuing renegotiation of the power that exists in the production and dissemination of nationhood as a cultural identity. Indeed, the images of the Chinese that we have examined reveal an important aspect of the modern nation: it exists in the very space of tension between articulations of ethnic and civic conceptualizations of nationhood. The result is a constant interplay and exchange of power between members of the nation that belie any definite boundary to nation space. In this sense, examining the representations of Chinese shop space in West Indian literature is an apt way of ending this study because the Chinese shop can be read as an important site from which the complex symbolic exchanges between villager and shopkeeper that gesture to the boundaries of nation occur.

It is often argued that in the West Indies, the Chinese shop, and more particularly, the counter therein, represents a fundamental divide between the Chinese and other members of the nation. Typical comments in this regard include the manner in which Victor Chang begins his conference paper, "'Counter Culture': The Chinese Shop in Jamaica." Chang posits that the shop counter is

> emblematic of the relationship which developed between the Chinese and the black Creole population: it was the site of the first sustained encounter between the cultures, the locus of their accounting with each other and the source of the peculiar dependency and hostility that have marked that relationship. Here . . . that counter was a barrier that had to be negotiated.[1]

Perceived as a site that is antagonistic to the needs and desires of other West Indians, Chinese shop space—particularly the space behind the counter—is depicted as a space of nonbelonging in the West Indies. This division is dramatically revealed in Samuel Selvon's *Turn Again Tiger* in the brief scene in which Tiger, Tall Boy, and Joe return to Tall Boy's shop after attending the fete that has symbolically integrated Tall Boy into the village community. When the men want more drinks, Tall Boy goes behind the counter. At this point his whole demeanor changes, as if, by entering the space behind the counter, he has entered a different dimension: "He switched on the lights and went behind the counter. Once there it was as if he had come into his element. His whole attitude changed, his voice took on a new note as he leaned over the counter and asked, 'What you having?'"[2]

But as suggested in Chang's description of "the peculiar dependence and hostility" of the Blacks and Chinese, the Chinese shop is more than a space of barriers, divisions, and alienation. It is also a site of important cultural transactions and exchange that create community life. Indeed, in many ways, West Indian literature represents the Chinese shop as an integral component of West Indian space. The plethora of Chinese shops scattered throughout West Indian literary texts certainly attests to this fact.[3] Additionally, the shop is often represented as being central to the lives of the community. Note, for example, the number of scenes that take place in Tall Boy's shop in the play "Highway in the Sun," a fact that suggests that shop space is actually representative of communal space in the village. On a very physical level, the shop space is where West Indian life survives, because it is the location of food and provisions. The shop is not, however, only a site of monetary exchange; rather, it is also the site of sociocultural exchanges that create new and specifically West Indian forms of life. As such, shop space becomes a site in which the nation is born and develops. Thus, for example, in *The Pagoda*, Lowe's shop is represented as a shared space of public domain in which all members of the community come together; it is the site where ideas and issues are discussed and protest groups are formed, where political ideas are developed, "the glassful of rum cocked in their hands and the heads close together."[4] Similarly, Lowe represents the shop as a place where life is "deposited" when he describes how the shop facilitates community building.

> [He had] lived there side by side with them. When drought struck and the land couldn't bear, hadn't he fed them? There wasn't one funeral he had missed. He locked shop early and attended every wedding with a box of hard-dough bread and a carton of white rum underneath his arm. He knew every child by name. He knew who was carrying belly for who. He knew who had money in the bank and who was working obeah for who. They left it all there in the shop.[5]

The Chinese shop, like West Indian literature in general, must therefore be recognized as a site of performance, that is, a site of contact and exchange between West Indians, where ideas of exclusion and inclusion, suspicion and trust, hostility and camaraderie—namely, ambiguous everyday ideas of belonging—are given tangible meaning through repetitive stylized gestures. Herein lies the significance of literary depictions of Chineseness to West Indian nationhood, for, as Butler might put it,

> This repetition is at once a re-enactment and re-experience of a set of meanings already socially established; and it is the mundane and ritualized form of their legitimization. . . . [National identity] ought not to be considered as a stable identity or locus of agency from which various acts follow; rather [it] is an identity tenuously constituted in time, instituted in an exterior space through a *stylized repetition of acts*.[6]

Admittedly—and perhaps most excitingly—the search for Mr. Chin is only just beginning. This book leaves many questions unanswered and points the way to future research possibilities that will undoubtedly complicate and expand our understanding of Chinese experience in the West Indies specifically and also in the wider Americas. We must, for example, begin to consider "the West Indies" and the Chinese of the West Indies in more heterogeneous terms: How was the experience of the Chinese different in Jamaica, Trinidad, and Guyana? Can we detect and account for differences in their cultural depictions? Were the experiences of the Chinese in the villages the same as for those in the towns? And where are all the Chinese women? Such study also provides opportunities for further interrogating the links and disconnections between the experiences and representations of the Chinese in the West Indies with other parts of the Americas—that is, of participating in a "hemispheric" exploration of Chineseness. In so doing, this work—this ongoing search for Mr. Chin—has the potential for giving us the exciting opportunity to radically "rewrite Asian American [and West Indian] history and challenge conventional understandings of migration, borders and globalization."[7]

Notes

Introduction

1. This book covers texts from both the colonial and the postcolonial periods from Jamaica, Trinidad, and Guyana. In recognition of this historical breadth, to maintain focus on these three regions rather than on the greater Caribbean, and for ease of reading, the term "West Indies" will be used rather than "Caribbean" when collectively referring to all three nations. For consistency, "Guyana" will be used instead of "British Guiana."

2. Arjun Appadurai, "Patriotism and Its Futures," *Public Culture* 5, no. 3 (1993): 411.

3. The new passport requirements came into effect on June 1, 2009.

4. Imre Szeman, *Zones of Instability: Literature, Postcolonialism, and the Nation* (Baltimore: Johns Hopkins University Press, 2003), 3.

5. Ibid., 6.

6. E. Stanley, *Claims and Resources of the West Indian Colonies: A Letter* (London: T. & W. Boone, 1850), 13, 35.

7. Letter to the Editor, *Royal Gazette*, 12 February 1850.

8. See Walton Look Lai's editorial note in *The Chinese in the West Indies, 1806–1995: A Documentary History* (Kingston: The Press University of the West Indies, 1998), 45. See also B. W. Higman, "The Chinese in Trinidad, 1806–1838" *Caribbean Studies* 12, no. 3 (1972): 21–44.

9. Cecil Clementi, *The Chinese in British Guiana* (Leeds: Derek Walcott Press in conjunction with Peepal Tree Press), 109.

10. John Edward Jenkins, *The Coolie: His Rights and Wrongs* (New York: George Routledge and Sons, 1871), 89–90.

11. For more detailed description of nineteenth-century Chinese inden-

tured labor migration, see Clementi, *The Chinese in British Guiana;* Persia Crawford Campbell, *Chinese Coolie Emigration to Countries within the British Empire* (London: P. S. King & Son, 1923); Jenkins, *The Coolie: His Rights and Wrongs;* Arnold J. Meagher, *The Coolie Trade: The Traffic in Chinese Laborers to Latin America, 1847–1874* (Philadelphia: Xlibris, 2008); and Walton Look Lai, *Indentured Labor, Caribbean Sugar: Chinese and Indian Migrants to the British West Indies, 1838–1918* (Baltimore: Johns Hopkins University Press, 1993) and *The Chinese in the West Indies, 1806–1995: A Documentary History* (Barbados, Jamaica, and Trinidad and Tobago: The Press University of the West Indies, 1998).

12. See also Lisa Yun's *The Coolie Speaks: Chinese Indentured Laborers and African Slaves in Cuba* (Philadelphia: Temple University Press, 2008).

13. See Meagher, *The Coolie Trade.*

14. From former magistrate G. W. Des Voeux's letter to Earl Granville, Colonial Secretary included as Appendix A in Jenkins, *The Coolie.*

15. Clementi, *The Chinese in British Guiana*, 127–128.

16. Ibid., 30.

17. Joseph Beaumont, *The New Slavery: An Account of the Indian and Chinese Immigrants in British Guiana* (London: W. Ridgway, 1871), 54.

18. Look Lai, *The Chinese in the West Indies*, 136, and Public Record Office (PRO) CO 295/222.

19. Jenkins, *The Coolie,* 155. The report of Low-A-Si's murder also appears in *The Coolie* on page 273.

20. Homi K. Bhabha, "Of Mimicry and Man," in *The Location of Culture* (London: Routledge, 2008), 122.

21. Editorial, *Royal Gazette*, 16 July 1853; Hislop to Windham, 26 October 1806, PRO CO 195/14; Editorial, *Royal Gazette*, 10 November 1870.

22. See Clementi, *The Chinese in British Guiana*, and Meagher, *The Coolie Trade,* for further details on the various Chinese mutinies during nineteenth-century labor migrations.

23. Look Lai, *The Chinese in the West Indies*, 23; Enclosed in Despatch from Walker to Newcastle, 8 July 1853, Parliamentary Papers (PP), vol. 68.

24. Jenkins, *The Coolie,* 54.

25. Minutes, PRO CO 295/14; "Report of Trinidad's Standing Committee"; Editorial, *Royal Gazette*, 16 July 1853.

26. Report of the Commissioners, PP, vol. 20 (also quoted in Jenkins, *The Coolie*, 298).

27. "The Heathen Chinee" was a popular nineteenth-century stereotype of the Chinese. The phrase was taken from Bret Harte's phenomenally successful poem "Plain Language from Truthful James," more popularly known by the title "The Heathen Chinee."

28. Barkly to Newcastle, 26 February 1853, PP, vol. 68.

29. Look Lai, *The Chinese in the West Indies*, 212, 218.

30. Editorial, *Royal Gazette*, 22 March 1870.

31. Bhabha, "Of Mimicry and Man," 123.

32. H. V. P. Bronkhurst, *British Guyana and Its Laboring Population* (London: T. Woolmer, 1883), 209, 254.

33. Charles Kingsley, *At Last: A Christmas in the West Indies* (London: Macmillan, 1889), 305.

34. Hislop, 16 April 1806, PRO CO 295/14.

35. Gloster to Marryat, 3 April 1807, PRO CO 295/14; Barkly to Grey, 26 August 1851, PP, vol. 68.

36. Report of the Commissioners, PP, vol. 20.

37. Editorial, *Royal Gazette*, 10 November 1870.

38. Editorial, *Royal Gazette*, 10 March 1874.

39. Edward Jenkins, *Lutchmee and Dilloo: A Study of West Indian Life in Three Volumes* (London: William Mullan & Son, 1877), 1:185.

40. Ibid., 1:204.

41. Ibid., 1:223.

42. Ibid., 3:68. "Tadja" is a Shiite Muslim festival commemorating the death of the grandson of Muhammad, Hussein. During the festival, large structures representing Hussein's tomb are constructed. The festival is also known as "Tadjah," "Tazia," or, in Trinidad, "Hosay."

43. Ibid., 1:22.

44. Edward Said, *Orientalism* (New York: Vintage Books Edition, 1979), 7.

45. Yun, *The Coolie Speaks,* xxiii.

1 / Forgotten Remembrance: Literature and the Banal Performance of Nation

1. See, for example, work by Etienne Balibar and Immanuel Wallerstein, Walker Connor, Ernest Gellner, Eric J. Hobsbawm, Thomas Hylland Eriksen, Elie Kedurie, and Anthony D. Smith.

2. Homi K. Bhabha, Introduction to *Nation and Narration* (New York: Routledge, 1990), 3.

3. Frantz Fanon, "On National Culture," in *The Wretched of the Earth*, trans. Constance Farrington (New York: Grove Press, 1963), 245.

4. Bhabha, Introduction to *Nation and Narration,* 1.

5. Timothy Brennan, "The National Longing for Form," in *Nation and Narration*, 48.

6. Bhabha, Introduction to *Nation and Narration,*1; Ernest Renan, "What Is a Nation?" in *Nation and Narration*, 19.

7. Homi K. Bhabha, "DissemiNation: Time Narrative and the Margins of the Modern Nation," in *Nation and Narration*, 297.

8. Ibid. 292.

9. Ibid. 294.

10. Bhabha, Introduction to *Nation and Narration,* 3.

11. Renan, "What Is a Nation?"19.

12. Bhabha, Introduction to *Nation and Narration,* 5; Renan, "What Is a Nation?" 11.

13. Regina Lee, "Theorizing Diasporas," in *Asian Diasporas: Cultures, Identities, Representations,* ed. Robbie B. H. Goh and Shawn Wong (Hong Kong: Hong Kong University Press 2004), 57.

14. Bhabha, Introduction to *Nation and Narration,* 1.

15. Lee, "Theorizing Diasporas," 57; Bhabha, Introduction to *Nation and Narration,* 4.

16. Lee, "Theorizing Diasporas," 56.

17. Lewis D. Wurgaf, "Identity in World History: A Postmodern Perspective," *History and Theory* 34, no. 2 (1995): 83.

18. Ibid., 84.

19. Hilary McD. Beckles, "Capitalism, Slavery and Caribbean Modernity," *Callaloo* 20, no. 4 (1998): 777, 785.

20. Manning Nash, "The Core Elements of Ethnicity," in *Ethnicity,* ed. John Hutchinson and Anthony D. Smith (Oxford: Oxford University Press, 1996), 25.

21. Anthony D. Smith, *National Identity* (London: Penguin, 1991), 15, 41.

22. *Norman Washington Manley and the New Jamaica: Selected Speeches and Writings, 1938–1968,* ed. Rex Nettleford (New York: Africana, 1971), 157, 100.

23. Cheddi Jagan, *Forbidden Freedom: The Story of British Guiana,* reprint (London: Hansib, 1989), 16.

24. Eric Williams, *Inward Hunger: The Education of a Prime Minister,* 2nd ed. (Chicago: University of Chicago Press, 1971), 232.

25. Both Anthony Trollope's *The West Indies and the Spanish Main* (1858; London: Frank Cass, 1968) and Thomas Carlyle's "Occasional Discourse on the Nigger Question," *Fraser's Magazine for Town and Country* 40 (1849) (accessed online at http://cepa.newshool.edu/het/texts/carlyle/carlodnq.htm, 12 April 2002), are saturated with images of the ex-slaves of the West Indies spending their days lying around and eating yams and pumpkins. Indeed, both men have been credited for popularization of the "Lazy Negro" stereotype so prevalent by the end of the nineteenth century.

26. Eric Williams, *History of the People of Trinidad and Tobago* (Port of Spain: PNM, 1962), 279.

27. Fanon, "On National Culture," 240.

28. Michael Billig, *Banal Nationalism* (London: Sage, 1995), 24.

29. Ibid., 6.

30. Fredric Jameson, "Third World Literature in the Era of Multinational Capitalism," *Social Text,* no. 15 (1986): 69.

31. Ibid.

32. Aijaz Ahmad, "Jameson's Rhetoric of Otherness and the 'National Allegory,'" *Social Text,* no. 17 (1987): 8–9.

33. Said, *Orientalism,* 20.

34. Bhabha, Introduction to *Nation and Narration*, 2.

35. Judith Butler, *The Judith Butler Reader*, ed. Sara Salih with Judith Butler (Malden, Mass.: Blackwell, 2004), 115.

36. Jeffrey C. Alexander, "Cultural Pragmatics: Social Performance between Ritual and Strategy," *Sociological Theory* 22, no. 4 (2004): 529.

37. Maureen Mahon, "The Visible Evidence of Cultural Producers," *Annual Review of Anthropology* 29 (2000): 467–468.

38. Alexander, "Cultural Pragmatics," 530, 532.

39. Karen A. Cerulo, *Identity Designs: The Sights and Sounds of a Nation* (New Brunswick, N.J.: Rutgers University Press, 1995), 3.

40. Alexander, "Cultural Pragmatics," 529.

2 / "Just Another Chinaman": The Chinese as Outsiders to the Nation

1. Said, *Orientalism*, 1.

2. Ibid.

3. Lisa Lowe, *Immigrant Acts: On Asian American Cultural Politics* (Durham, N.C.: Duke University Press, 1996), 4.

4. Ibid., 2, 12.

5. Elaine H. Kim, "'Such Opposite Creatures': Men and Women in Asian American Literature," *Michigan Quarterly* 29, no. 1 (1990): 70; Said, *Orientalism*, 7.

6. Said, *Orientalism*, 1, 2.

7. Ignacio López-Calvo, *Imaging the Chinese in Cuban Literature and Culture* (Gainesville: University Press of Florida, 2008), 62.

8. For example, in her work on Octavio Paz, Julia Kushigian points to the river and to the Möbius strip in Sarduy's work as symbolic of this blending of opposites. See "'Ríos en la noche: Fluyen los jardines': Orientalism in the Work of Octavio Paz," *Hispania* 70, no. 4 (1987): 776–786.

9. López-Calvo, *Imaging the Chinese in Cuban Literature and Culture*, 62.

10. Lancelot Cowie, "Chinese in Contemporary Cuban Narrative," in *Essays on the Chinese Diaspora in the Caribbean*, ed. Walton Look Lai (St. Augustine, Trinidad: History Department, University of the West Indies, 2006), 146.

11. In "Men in the Yard and On the Street: Cricket and Calypso in Moon on a Rainbow Shawl and Miguel Street," *Anthurium: A Caribbean Studies Journal* 3, no. 2 (2005), for example, Claire Westall points to the significance of masculinity when she argues that the characters struggle with the belief that "'man-ness' will lead the people to freedom, liberty and, crucially, Nationhood."

12. V. S. Naipaul, *Miguel Street* (London: Penguin, 1959), 14.

13. Alecia McKenzie's short story "Jakes Makes" (in *Satellite City and Other Stories* [Essex: Longman Group UK, 1992], 54–78) uses a similar incident to depict Jamaica as a sterile environment for Black men in terms of emotional and financial productivity. In this story, Jakes' girlfriend becomes

pregnant by her boss, Mr. Chang, although she initially claims that paternity belongs to Jakes.

14. Ibid., 66.

15. Elizabeth Nunez, *Bruised Hibiscus* (New York: Ballantine Books, 2000); Sylvia Wynter, *The Hills of Hebron* (Essex: Longman Group, 1984). Interestingly, there are few images of Chinese women as sexual beings in West Indian literature, perhaps due at least partially to the fact that there are very few depictions of Chinese women at all. The most common image of Chinese women in West Indian literature is of women working next to their shopkeeper husbands and raising their children. Examples of this common image appear in stories such as Noel Woodroffe's "Wing's Way," in *Best West Indian Stories*, ed. Kenneth Ramchand (Surrey: Thomas Nelson and Sons, 1984), 138–144, and Samuel Selvon's *A Brighter Sun* (Essex: Pearson, 1985).

A notable exception to this rule is the scene in Roger Mais' *The Hills Were Joyful Together* (Kingston and Port of Spain: Heinemann, 1981) when Manny recounts his sexual exploits with the apparently promiscuous daughter of the Chinese shopkeeper referred to only as "Squiz Eye." Wilfie's response to Manny's story is to make the following comment about Chinese women: "An' the thing turned cross-ways, they say" (19). His statement suggests that there is something perceived to be unnatural or even hideously monstrous about "Squiz Eye" that could be read as being just as threatening to her Black male lovers as the male shopkeeper is often imagined to be in his relationship with village women in West Indian literature.

16. Selvon, *A Brighter Sun,* 59.

17. Nunez, *Bruised Hibiscus,* 89.

18. Ibid., 90–91.

19. A typical example of such an attitude is evident in an 1889 Trinidadian newspaper article's description of Chinese shopkeepers as "horseleeches, or . . . a parasite which settles on a plant not vigorous enough to throw it off, and which it saps of its strength" (as quoted in Howard Johnson's "The Chinese in Trinidad in the Late Nineteenth Century," *Ethnic and Racial Studies* 10, no. 1 [1987]: 88).

20. Portuguese shopkeepers were, however, the target of riots that occurred in Guyana in 1856 and 1889.

21. The image of the Chinese shopkeeper as an exploiter and oppressor of other members of the nation is a common stereotype that appears throughout West Indian literature, including, for example, the depictions of Hoo, Chin Toon, and Yankee in Ralph de Boissière's *Crown Jewel* (Suffolk: Richard Clay, 1981); "them money-hungry Chinese shopmen" in Monar Rooplall's "Money Can't Play" (in *Estate People* [Georgetown: Roraima, 1994], 51–57); and the shopkeeper that Tansy encounters in Mais' *The Hills Were Joyful Together.*

22. V. S. Naipaul, *Guerrillas* (London: André Deutsch, 1975), 27.

23. Ibid., 23.

24. Ibid., 143.

25. Patricia Powell, *The Pagoda* (San Diego: Harcourt Brace, 1998), 15.

26. Ibid., 13.

27. Ibid., 73.

28. Alfred Mendes, *Black Fauns* (London: New Beacon Books, 1984), 123. A "barrack-yard" is an urban slum or shanty town. Similar sentiments are expressed by numerous characters throughout West Indian literature, including, for example, Samuel Selvon's "Highway in the Sun" (in *Highway in the Sun: A Collection of Plays* [Leeds: Peepal Tree Press, 1991]) and Alecia McKenzie's "Stuck in the Maid's Room" (in *Satellite City and Other Stories* [Essex: Longman Group UK, 1992]). Indeed, McKenzie's story emphasizes the image of the Chinese as interested only in what they can make off of other West Indians when it creates the memorable image of members of the Jamaican Chinese community fleeing the country with suitcases overflowing with money when a new socialist-leaning government comes into power.

29. Naipaul, *Miguel Street*, 85.

30. Samuel Selvon, "Song of Sixpence," in *The Penguin Book of Caribbean Short Stories*, ed. E. A. Markham (London: Penguin, 1996), 138.

31. Eric Walrond, "The Wharf Rats," in *The Penguin Book of Caribbean Short Stories*, 101.

32. McKenzie's "Stuck in the Maid's Room" provides another dramatic image of the Chinese community as outsiders to the national community by portraying the Chinese as distanced from the discourse used to construct national belonging. Specifically, the political rhetoric in fashion at the time of this story deems it incorrect to call one's "brothers and sisters" "maids." The fact that the members of the Chinese community continue to call their domestic assistants "maids" clearly positions them outside of the "national family."

33. Alfred Mendes, "Her Chinaman's Way," in *From Trinidad: An Anthology of Early West Indian Writing*, ed. Reinhard W. Sander (Kent: Hodder and Stoughton, 1978), 108.

34. Ibid., 105.

35. Ibid., 114.

36. Ibid., 104.

37. Edgar Mittelholzer, *A Morning in the Office* (London: Heinemann, 1974), 209.

38. Other examples of a seeming social flexibility allowed to the Chinese as outsiders to West Indian social hierarchies include San Tie's seeming ability to move from laboring camps, to bush, to city life, as well as between sexual identities in "The Wharf Rats," and the White Creole Sally's willingness to date Dave Chow in *Pan Beat*, although "she would never have the courage to go around with colored boys" (39). Additionally, Chinese shop space is sometimes depicted as a space that is outside the confines of conventional ideas of West Indian respectability. In Deryck M. Bernard's "Ben," the

casual social freedoms found in the Chinese shop are contrasted with the rigid confines of respectability demanded in Aunt Hildred's shop. A similar vision of the Chinese shop also appears in Olive Senior's "The Tenantry of Birds" when Noelene notes that her socially ambitious mother would never patronize a Chinese shop. Significantly, it is only in Chinese shop space that Noelene feels free from the demands of her mother's "respectability," or as Noelene puts it, only in the shop does she feel as if there is no one looking over her shoulder (51).

39. Naipaul, *Guerrillas*, 205–206.

40. de Boissière, *Crown Jewel*,188.

41. Ibid., 191. Chin Toon is not unique. The image of Chinese characters who are alienated from West Indian political interests is common through West Indian literature. For example, in N. D. Williams' *Ikael Torass* (Havana: Casa de las Américas, 1976), not only does the Chinese shopkeeper lock up his cash register at the first sign of trouble, but Precious, the part-Chinese freshman, never participates in any student protests. In Michael Reckford's "Dog Food," the Chinese grocery manager's emotional distance from the rioters is symbolized by the fact that his office is on an elevated platform separated from the mob and in his ability to discuss business as usual with the unnamed narrator despite the turmoil and distress around them.

42. The burning alive of a policeman fictionalized in *Crown Jewel* is based on a real incident that occurred in the labor unrest of 1930s Trinidad. In Michael Anthony's rewriting of the same incident, "Butler on the Road," the Chinese shopkeeper is depicted as hiding beneath the shop counter when the mob enters the shop.

43. Naipaul, *Guerrillas*, 189.

44. See, for example, Anne R. Zahlan's "Literary Murder: V. S. Naipaul's *Guerrillas*," *South Atlantic Review* 59, no. 4 (1994): 89–106, and Hana Wirth-Nesher's "The Cause of Marginality: Colonialism in Naipaul's *Guerrillas*," *Modern Fiction Studies* 30, no. 3 (1984): 531–545.

45. Naipaul, *Guerrillas*, 207.

46. Zahlan, "Literary Murder," 91.

47. Naipaul, *Guerrillas*, 39–40, 62.

48. Ibid., 141.

49. Zahlan, "Literary Murder," 98.

50. Naipaul, *Guerrillas*, 191.

51. Ibid. 17.

52. Ibid.

53. Ibid., 198–199.

54. Marion Patrick Jones, *Pan Beat* (Port of Spain: Columbus, 1973), 154.

55. Ibid., 28.

56. Ibid., 3. "Pan" is the short form for "steelpan" (sometimes referred to as a "steeldrum"), a percussion musical instrument originally constructed

out of an oil drum. Although initially it was considered "lower class" by many Trinidadians, it is now embraced as the national instrument of Trinidad and Tobago.

57. William York Tindall, "The Sociological Best Seller," *College English* 9, no. 2 (1947): 58.

58. Robert Standish, *Mr. On Loong* (London: Peter Davies, 1950), 88.

59. Ibid., 91.

60. Ibid., 247.

61. *Norman Washington Manley and the New Jamaica*, 110.

62. H. Lynch-Campbell, *Chinese in Jamaica* (Kingston: City Printery, 1975), 94.

3 / "A Real Creolise Chinee": Establishing Creole Inclusiveness

1. See, for example, Michael Billig's discussion on national identity in *Banal Nationalism* and Cerulo's *Identity Designs*.

2. The word "creole" has a variety of inflections throughout the Caribbean. In the Hispanic Caribbean, "creole" often refers specifically to individuals who are of European descent but have had a long ancestral presence in the Caribbean. In the French Caribbean, "creole" is generally used to describe the specific French dialect developed in the islands such that for "Créolistes" such as Jean Bernabé, Patrick Chamoiseau, and Raphaël Confiant, "créolité" is most importantly an art aesthetic in which language is the central component; that is, they posit understandings of "creole" and "creolization" as "an open specificity" and "*the interactional or transactional aggregate* of Caribbean, European, African, Asian and Levantine cultural elements, united on the same soil by the yoke of history," but also argue that it is through the language of French creole that créolité finds its truest expression.

3. Stuart Hall, "Culture and Identity," in *Theorizing Diaspora*, ed. Jana Evans Braziel and Anita Mannur (Malden, Mass.: Blackwell, 2003), 236, 237.

4. Ibid., 243.

5. Ibid., 243, 244.

6. These are the Plantation and Plural Models. Brathwaite specifies the distinction between his creole theory and "the classic plural society paradigm" when he writes: "The classic plural society paradigm is based on an apprehension of cultural polarity, on an 'either/or' principle, on the idea of people sharing common divisions instead of increasingly common values. My own idea of creolization is based on the notion of an historically affected socio-cultural continuum" (Kamau Brathwaite, *The Development of Creole Society in Jamaica, 1770–1820* [Kingston: Ian Randle, 2005], 310).

7. Ibid., 296.

8. Ibid., 309, 311.

9. *Norman Washington Manley and the New Jamaica*, 109, 159.

10. Forbes Burnham, *A Destiny to Mould: Selected Speeches by the Prime*

Minister of Guyana, compiled by C. A. Nascimento and R. A. Burrowes (New York: Africana, 1970), 149.

11. Percy C. Hintzen, "Race and Creole Ethnicity in the Caribbean," in *Questioning Creole: Creolisation Discourses in Caribbean Culture,* ed. Verene A. Shepherd and Glen L. Richards (Kingston: Ian Randle; and Oxford: James Currey, 2002), 92.

12. Brathwaite, *The Development of Creole Society in Jamaica,* 310, 307. Brathwaite consciously marginalizes the contribution of other ethnic groups to Jamaican-creole society when he excludes them from his list of the four "orientations" of Jamaican creole culture. Although he specifically indicates that "The 'East Indian' problem" is not included "since it introduces new complexities, and does not (yet) significantly relate to Jamaica" (310), the Chinese community of Jamaica does not even merit mention.

13. Hintzen, "Race and Creole Ethnicity in the Caribbean," 99. A particular awareness of the "blackening" of creole nationalism is apparent in Trinidad where the presence of Indo-Trinidadians has numerically challenged Afro-West Indians. See Ivar Oxaal's *Black Intellectuals Come to Power: The Rise of Creole Nationalism in Trinidad and Tobago* (Cambridge: Schenkman, 1968), and "The Culture of Williams: Context, Performance, Legacy," *Callaloo* 20, no. 4 (1997): 849–888.

14. Amaryll Chanady, "From Difference to Exclusion: Multiculturalism and Postcolonialism," *International Journal of Politics, Culture, and Society* 8, no. 3 (1995): 427. This article provides a thorough summary of much of the debates in this area.

15. Juan de Castro, *Mestizo Nations: Culture, Race, and Conformity in Latin American Literature* (Tucson: University of Arizona Press, 2002) as quoted in López-Calvo, *Imaging the Chinese in Cuban Literature and Culture,* 23. The concept of *mestizo* nations does, however, focus more explicitly on the idea of mixed bloods, particularly European-Indigenous mixing, than is done so in theoretical articulations of "creole."

16. Ibid., 21.

17. Hall, "Culture and Identity," 244.

18. Samuel Selvon, *Turn Again Tiger* (Port of Spain and Kingston: Heinemann. n.d.), 14–15.

19. Ibid., 15. So important is this moment for Selvon in terms of establishing belonging for his Chinese characters in the nation that Selvon reinscribes this scene in "Highway in the Sun," even though the play is actually more of a dramatization of *A Brighter Sun* than *Turn Again Tiger.* Also different is the fact that in the play, the party is a celebration for the birth of Tiger and Urmilla's daughter instead of a good-bye party; however, just as in *Turn Again Tiger,* Tall Boy is omitted from the guest list and must invite himself. In the play, Urmilla's lack of surprise when Tall Boy announces his intention of attending the fete demonstrates that she already considers Tall Boy a full member of their village community in

much the same way as the guests' lack of reaction to Tall Boy's appearance at the party in the novel.

20. Ibid.

21. Ibid., 16.

22. Michael Anthony, "Many Things," in *Cricket in the Road* (Oxford: Heinemann, 1973), 67.

23. Ibid., 66.

24. See, for example, Ernest Gellner's discussion of the development of "high culture" in *Nations and Nationalism* (Ithaca, N.Y.: Cornell University Press, 1983).

25. Helen Atteck, *Bound for Trinidad: An Historical Novel* (St. Catharines: Wanata, 2004), 110.

26. Selvon, *A Brighter Sun*, 55.

27. In a similar fashion, Bernadette Gabay Dyer's *Waltzes I Have Not Forgotten* (Toronto: Women's Press, 2004) suggests the complex and cosmopolitan atmosphere of both Kingston, Jamaica, and London, England, by including the presence of the Chinese.

28. Alecia McKenzie, "The Grenada Defense League," in *Satellite City and Other Stories*, 141.

29. Mittelholzer, *A Morning in the Office*, 208.

30. Hall, "Culture and Identity," 243, 244.

31. Ibid., 240.

32. Margaret Cezair-Thompson, *The True History of Paradise* (New York: Random House, 2009), 78.

33. Hall, "Culture and Identity," 244.

34. Cezair-Thompson, *The True History of Paradise*, 17.

35. Ibid., 25.

36. Ibid., 296.

37. Ibid., 254.

38. Ibid., 41, 42.

39. Ibid., 197.

40. Ibid., 9.

41. See Howard Johnson, "The Anti-Chinese Riots of 1918 in Jamaica," *Caribbean Quarterly* 28, no. 3 (1982): 19–32.

42. Cezair-Thompson, *The True History of Paradise*, 80.

43. Nunez, *Bruised Hibiscus*, 6.

44. Ibid., 7.

45. Ibid., 8.

46. Ibid., 117.

47. Selvon, "Highway in the Sun," 12.

48. Ibid., 32.

49. McKenzie, "Jakes Makes," 64.

50. Paule Marshall, "British Guiana," in *Soul Clap Hands and Sing* (Washington, D.C.: Howard University Press, 1988), 103.

51. Ibid., 74.
52. Ibid., 75.
53. McKenzie, "Jakes Makes," 66, 62.
54. Ibid., 66.
55. Similarly, in *Miguel Street*, Eddoes' part-Chinese "daughter" also becomes a beauty contest winner.
56. Alfred Mendes, *Pitch Lake* (London: New Beacon Books, 1980), 88.
57. Mendes, "Her Chinaman's Way," 104, 105.
58. Williams, *Ikael Torass*, 143.
59. Marshall, "British Guiana," 95.
60. Woodroffe, "Wing's Way," 144.
61. Wynter, *The Hills of Hebron*, 185.
62. López-Calvo, *Imaging the Chinese in Cuban Literature and Culture*, 152.
63. Hall, "Culture and Identity," 236.
64. Cezair-Thompson, *The True History of Paradise*, 78.

4 / From the Other Side of the Counter: Chinese West Indian Self-Representation

1. Frantz Fanon, "The Fact of Blackness," in *Black Skin, White Masks*, trans. Charles Lam Markmann (London: Pluto Press, 1986), 111, 110.
2. Ien Ang, "Can One Say No to Chineseness? Pushing the Limits of the Diasporic Paradigm," *boundary 2* 25, no. 3 (1998): 239.
3. Standish, *Mr. On Loong*, 133, 185–186.
4. Powell, *The Pagoda*, 33.
5. V. S. Naipaul, "The Baker's Story," in *The Penguin Book of Caribbean Short Stories*, 173.
6. A similar phenomenon has been noticed in Cuba.
7. E-mail from Willi Chen to Anne-Marie Lee-Loy, 3 August 2002. In an interview with Stewart Brown ("Stewart Brown Interviews Willi Chen, Author of *The King of the Carnival* (Hansib, 1988)," *Journal of West Indian Literature* 51, no. 1/2 [1992]: 106–112), Chen indicated that he does not write about Chinese West Indian experience because he believes that the older Chinese population, from whose experience he would like to draw on, are dying off or "becoming senile." His comments are particularly interesting in terms of this study because they suggest that Chen has not seriously considered his own experiences as a valid expression of Chineseness in the West Indies.
8. Conversation with Easton Lee, Kingston, Jamaica, 12 July 2002.
9. David Palumbo-Liu, "The Minority Self as Other: Problematics of Representation in Asian American Literature," *Cultural Critique*, no. 28 (1994): 88.
10. Ibid., 90 and 96.
11. López-Calvo, *Imaging the Chinese in Cuban Literature and Culture*, 80.

12. Liu, "The Minority Self as Other," 100.

13. Victor Chang, "Light in the Shop," *Small Axe*, no. 2 (1997): 105.

14. "Stewart Brown Interviews Willi Chen," 107.

15. Ibid., 111.

16. Victor Chang, "'Counter Culture': The Chinese Shop in Jamaica" (unpublished, presented at the Toronto Hakka Heritage and Culture Conference, York University, Toronto, Ontario, 29 and 30 December 2000), 2.

17. Conversation with Victor Chang, Kingston, Jamaica, 12 July 2002.

18. Easton Lee, "One Day," in *From Behind the Counter*, 9.

19. Lee, "Friday," 2.

20. Lee, "All Week," 11.

21. Chang, "Light in the Shop," 104.

22. Ibid.

23. Lee, "Some Days," in *From Behind the Counter*, 6.

24. For example, none of the shop poems in Lee's *From Behind the Counter* collection refers to "our shop" or describe the shops with personal pronouns such as "mine" or "my."

25. Lee, "Everyday," 6.

26. Lee, "Next Day," 8.

27. Lee, "Every Night" and "Some Nights," 12, 13.

28. Chang, "Light in the Shop," 104.

29. Ibid., 108.

30. Easton Lee, "Language Class," in *Heritage Call: Ballad for the Children of the Dragon* (Kingston: Ian Randle, 2001), 75.

31. Ibid.

32. Easton Lee, "Birthday Song," in *From Behind the Counter*, 41.

33. Lee, "One World," in *Heritage Call*, 77.

34. In *Mirror, Mirror: Identity, Race, and Protest in Jamaica* (Kingston: William Collins and Sangster, 1970), Rex Nettleford provides this well-known (and limited) construct of Jamaican space: "Europe and Africa . . . [forming] . . . an organic whole inextricably bound up and expressive of a new and rich phenomenon which is neither Africa nor Europe, yet embodying the two in unprecedented and creative modes of relationship" (173).

35. Elaine H. Kim, "Defining Asian American Realities through Literature," *Cultural Critique*, no. 6 (1987): 88.

36. "Stewart Brown Interviews Willi Chen," 108.

37. Rey Chow, Introduction to *Writing Diaspora: Tactics of Intervention in Contemporary Cultural Studies* (Bloomington: Indiana University Press, 1993), 17.

38. Ibid., 16

39. Ibid., 17.

40. Ibid.

41. Ibid.

42. Chow, *Writing Diaspora*, 24.

43. Ang, "Can One Say No to Chineseness?" 241.

44. Janice Shinebourne, *Timepiece* (Leeds: Peepal Tree Press, n.d.), 153.

45. Ibid., 26, 55.

46. Meiling Jin, "Victoria," in *Song of the Boatwoman* (Leeds: Peepal Tree Press, 1996), 7.

47. Ibid. In the Berbice region of Guyana, the green fruit of the calabash tree is sometimes referred to colloquially as "goobi." Using the term in this case highlights the absolute worthlessness of the Chinese life; that is, it is as worthless as a common fruit.

48. Ibid., 11.

49. Ibid., 10.

50. Janice Shinebourne, *The Last English Plantation* (Leeds: Peepal Tree Press, 1988), 37.

51. Ibid., 100–101.

52. Ibid., 150.

53. Ibid., 61.

54. Ibid., 74. A "bacoo" is an evil spirit in Guyanese folklore. When used as an insult, the term expresses ideas of ugliness and of being uncivilized.

55. Jin, "Short Fuse," in *Song of the Boatwoman*, 89.

56. Shinebourne, *Timepiece*, 34.

57. Ibid., 36.

58. Ibid., 74. In contrast, what initially attracts Sandra to Son is the fact that he seems to have freed himself from the space of male aggression and domination established for him in his society. Son's relationship with Sandra is described in the following manner: "[H]e did not want to contest a position with her. . . . That he was a man unafraid of a woman—this was a stronger ground for trust. He did not depend on male group identity. His being was not in opposition" (146–147).

59. Ibid., 37.

60. In *Timepiece*, Paul once tries to end an argument with Sandra by telling her, "You women don't understand these things," to which Sandra responds, "That's supposed to be my cross?" (100). Sandra's response suggests that in Guyana, womanhood is a burden—a cross to bear.

61. Shinebourne, *The Last English Plantation*, 128.

62. Shinebourne, *Timepiece*, 36.

63. Ibid., 37; Shinebourne, *The Last English Plantation*, 101.

64. Jin, "Victoria," 12.

65. Ibid., 12, 15.

66. Shinebourne, *The Last English Plantation*, 128.

67. Shinebourne, *Timepiece*, 48.

68. Ibid., 125.

69. Ibid., 153, 156.

70. Shinebourne, *The Last English Plantation*, 16.

71. Ibid., 171.

72. Shinebourne, *Timepiece*, 153.

73. Shinebourne, *The Last English Plantation*, 72.

74. Ibid.

75. Stuart Hall, "New Ethnicities," in *Black British Cultural Studies: A Reader*, ed. Houston A. Baker Jr., Manthia Diawara, and Ruth H. Lindeborg (Chicago: University of Chicago Press, 1996), 166.

76. Ang, "Can One Say No to Chineseness?" 242.

77. A subtle, yet significant, conceptual difference is revealed in Chang and Lee's definitions of the phrase "eleven o'clock children" that points to the many-layered conceptualizations of Chineseness in the West Indies. Chang's translation is more restrictive than Lee's; Chang applies the term only to those who are "of pure Chinese stock" ("Light in the Shop," 104). In contrast, Lee suggests that the description applies to any child of a Chinese migrant born in Jamaica, and, by doing so, he includes children who may have a parent who is not of Chinese ethnicity (Preface to *Heritage Call*, 9–10).

78. Chang, "Light in the Shop," 104.

79. Ibid., 107.

80. Janice Shinebourne, "The Berbice Marriage Match," in *The Godmother and Other Stories* (Leeds: Peepal Tree Press, 2004), 107; Ang, "Can One Say No to Chineseness?" 223.

81. Shinebourne, "The Berbice Marriage Match," 107.

82. Ibid., 109.

83. Ibid., 109, 110.

84. Chow, *Writing Diaspora*, 24.

85. Shinebourne, *Timepiece* 153.

86. Hall, "New Ethnicities," 163–164.

87. In contrast, in Jin's "Short Fuse," Gladys claims access to a specific Chinese identity only when reading about the violent racial conflicts occurring in Guyana. In this story the value in Chineseness is that it distances Gladys from the growing violence and antagonism "back home" and allows her the safety of claiming neutral space. This is most evident in the moment when, reading her husband's description of the events in Guyana, Gladys declares: "Black against East Indian and we Chiney in between" (96).

88. Shinebourne, "The Berbice Marriage Match," 111.

89. Ang, "Can One Say No to Chineseness?" 239.

90. Shinebourne, "London and New York," in *The Godmother and Other Stories*, 98.

91. Ibid., 96.

92. Ibid.

93. Ibid., 100.

94. Ibid., 100–101.

95. Ibid., 99.

96. Ibid.

Conclusion

1. Chang, "Counter Culture," 1.
2. Selvon, *Turn Again Tiger*, 17.
3. So embedded is the presence of "the Chinese shop" in the imaginative landscape of the West Indies that it would be impossible to provide a comprehensive list of all the texts that make reference to the shop in all its forms, including, for example, haberdasheries, restaurants, bakeries, tea rooms, and cafés.
4. Powell, *The Pagoda*, 32.
5. Ibid., 39
6. Butler, *The Judith Butler Reader*, 114.
7. Erika Lee, "Orientalisms in the Americas: A Hemispheric Approach to Asian American History," *Journal of Asian American Studies* 8, no. 3 (2005): 251.

Selected Bibliography

Adamson, Alan H. "The Impact of Indentured Immigration on the Political Economy of British Guiana." In *Indentured Labor in the British Empire, 1834–1920,* edited by Kay Saunders, 42–56. London: Croom Helm, 1984.

Ahmad, Aijaz. "Jameson's Rhetoric of Otherness and the 'National Allegory.'" *Social Text,* no. 17 (1987): 3–25.

Alexander, Jeffrey C. "Cultural Pragmatics: Social Performance between Ritual and Strategy." *Sociological Theory* 22, no. 4 (2004): 527–573.

Anderson, Benedict. *Imagined Communities: Reflections on the Origin and Spread of Nationalism.* New York: Verso, 1983.

Ang, Ien. "Can One Say No to Chineseness? Pushing the Limits of the Diasporic Paradigm." *boundary 2* 25, no. 3 (1998): 223–242.

Anthony, Michael. "Butler on the Road." In *The Chieftain's Carnival and Other Stories,* 143–161. Essex: Longman Group, 1993.

———. "Many Things." In *Cricket on the Road,* 66–71. Oxford: Heinemann, 1973.

———. "The Village Shop." In *Cricket in the Road,* 115–120.

Appadurai, Arjun. "Patriotism and Its Futures." *Public Culture* 5, no. 3 (1993): 411–429.

Atteck, Helen. *Bound for Trinidad: An Historical Novel.* St. Catharines, Ont.: Wanata, 2004.

Atteck, Helen, and Philip Atteck. *Stress of Weather: A Collection of*

Original Source Documents Relating to a Voyage from China to Trinidad, West Indies in 1862 in Conjunction with a Family Chronicle. St. Catharines, Ont.: Wanata, 1999.

Balibar, Étienne. "The Nation Form: History and Ideology." In *Race, Nation, Class: Ambiguous Identities* by Étienne Balibar and Immanuel Wallerstein, translated by Chris Turner, 86–106. London: Verso, 1991.

———. "Racism and Nationalism." In *Race, Nation, Class: Ambiguous Identities,* 37–67.

Barrett, William Garland. *Immigration to the British West Indies: Is it the Slave-Trade Revived or Not?* London: A. W. Bennett, 1859.

Beaumont, Joseph. *The New Slavery: An Account of the Indian and Chinese Immigrants in British Guiana.* London: W. Ridgway, 1871.

Beckles, Hilary McD. "Capitalism, Slavery and Caribbean Modernity." *Callaloo* 20, no. 4 (1998): 777–789.

Benn, Denis M. "The Theory of Plantation Economy and Society: A Methodological Critique." *Journal of Commonwealth and Comparative Politics* 12, no. 3 (1974): 249–260.

Bernabé, Jean, Patrick Chamoiseau, and Raphaël Confiant. "In Praise of Creoleness." Translated by Mohammed B. Taleb Khyar. *Callaloo* 13, no. 4 (1990): 869–909.

Bernard, Deryck M. "Ben." In *Going Home and Other Tales from Guyana,* 1–5. Oxford: Macmillan, 2002.

Best, Lloyd A. "The Mechanism of Plantation-Type Economies: Outlines of a Model of Pure Plantation Economy." *Social and Economic Studies* 17, no. 3 (1968): 283–397.

Bhabha, Homi K. "DissemiNation: Time, Narrative and the Margins of the Modern Nation." In *Nation and Narration,* edited by Homi K. Bhabha, 291–322. New York: Routledge, 1990.

———. "Introduction: Narrating the Nation." In *Nation and Narration,* 3–7.

———. "Of Mimicry and Man: The Ambivalence of Colonial Discourse." In *The Location of Culture,* 121–131. London: Routledge, 1994.

———. "The Other Question: Stereotype Discrimination and the Discourse of Colonialism." In *The Location of Culture,* 66–84.

Billig, Michael. *Banal Nationalism.* London: Sage, 1995.

Bolland, O. Nigel. "Creolisation and Creole Societies: A Cultural Nationalist View of Caribbean Social History." In *Questioning Creole,* edited by Verene A. Shepherd and Glen L. Richards, 15–46. Kingston: Ian Randle; Oxford: James Currey, 2002.

Brathwaite, Kamau. *The Development of Creole Society in Jamaica, 1770–1820.* Kingston: Ian Randle, 2005.

Brennan, Timothy. "The National Longing for Form." In *Nation and Narration,* edited by Bhabha, 44–70.

Bronkhurst, H. V. P. *British Guyana and Its Laboring Population.* London: T. Woolmer, 1883.

Bryan, Patrick. "The Creolization of the Chinese Community in Jamaica." In *Ethnic Minorities in Caribbean Societies,* edited by Rhoda E. Reddock, 173–271. St. Augustine, Trinidad: University of the West Indies, 1996.

Burnham, Forbes. *A Destiny to Mould: Selected Speeches by the Prime Minister of Guyana.* Compiled by C. A. Nascimento and R. A. Burrowes. New York: Africana, 1970.

Carlyle, Thomas. "Occasional Discourse on the Negro Question." *Fraser's Magazine for Town and Country* XL (1849), accessed online at http://cepa.newshool.edu/het/texts/carlyle/carlodnq.htm as of 15 May 2002.

Cerulo, Karen A. *Identity Designs: The Sights and Sounds of a Nation.* New Brunswick, N.J.: Rutgers University Press, 1995.

Cezair-Thompson, Margaret. *The True History of Paradise.* New York: Random House, 2009.

Chamoiseau, Patrick, Raphaël Confiant, Jean Bernabé, and Lucien Taylor. "Créolité Bites" (in conversation). *Transition,* no. 75 (1997): 124–161.

Chan, Jachinson. *Chinese American Masculinities: From Fu Manchu to Bruce Lee.* New York: Routledge, 2001.

Chanady, Amaryll. "From Difference to Exclusion: Multiculturalism and Postcolonialism." *International Journal of Politics, Culture and Society* 8, no. 3 (1995): 419–437.

Chang, Carlisle. "Chinese in Trinidad Carnival." *Drama Review* 42, no. 3 (1998): 213–219.

Chang, Victor. "'Counter Culture': The Chinese Shop in Jamaica." Unpublished, presented at the Toronto Hakka Heritage and Culture Conference, York University, Toronto, Ontario, 29 and 30 December 2000.

Chen, Willi. *Chutney Power.* Oxford: Macmillan Caribbean, 2006.

———. *King of the Carnival and Other Stories.* London: Hansib, 1988.

Chow, Rey. "Introduction: On Chineseness as a Theoretical Problem." *boundary 2* 25, no. 3 (1998): 1–24.

———. *Writing Diaspora: Tactics of Intervention in Contemporary Cultural Studies.* Bloomington: Indiana University Press, 1993.

Chun, Allen. "Fuck Chineseness: On the Ambiguities of Ethnicity as Culture as Identity." *boundary 2* 23, no. 2 (1996): 111–138.

Clementi, Cecil. *The Chinese in British Guiana.* Leeds: Derek Walcott Press, 2009.

Cmiel, Kenneth. "The Fate of the Nation and the Withering of the State." *American Literary History* 8, no. 1 (1996): 184–202.

Cowie, Lancelot. "Chinese in Contemporary Cuban Narrative." In *Essays on the Chinese Diaspora in the Caribbean,* edited by Walton Look Lai, 130–152. St. Augustine, Trinidad: History Department, University of the West Indies, 2006.

Crawford Campbell, Persia. *Chinese Coolie Emigration to Countries within the British Empire.* London: P. S. King & Son, 1923.

Cross, Malcolm. "Cultural Pluralism and Sociological Theory: A Critique and Re-evaluation." *Social and Economic Studies* 17, no. 4 (1968): 381–397.

Croucher, Sheila L. "Perpetual Imagining: Nationhood in a Global Era." *International Studies Review* 5, no. 1 (2003): 1–24.

de Boissière, Ralph. *Crown Jewel.* Suffolk: Richard Clay (The Chaucer Press), 1981.

Despres, Leo A. *Cultural Pluralism and Nationalist Politics in British Guiana.* Chicago: Rand McNally, 1967.

Des Voeux, G. W. *My Colonial Service in British Guiana, St. Lucia, Trinidad, Fiji, Australia, Newfoundland and Hong Kong with Interludes.* Vol. 1. London: John Murray, 1903.

Dorsey, Joseph C. "Identity, Rebellion, and Social Justice among Chinese Contract Workers in Nineteenth-Century Cuba." *Latin American Perspectives* 31, no. 3 (2004): 18–47.

Downey, Dennis J. "From Americanization to Multiculturalism: Political Symbols and Struggle for Cultural Diversity in Twentieth-Century American Race Relations." *Sociological Perspectives* 42, no. 2 (1999): 249–278.

During, Simon. "Literature—Nationalism's Other? The Case for Revision." In *Nation and Narration,* ed. Bhabha, 138–153.

Dyer, Bernadette Gabay. *Waltzes I Have Not Forgotten.* Toronto: Women's Press, 2004.

Eng, David L. *Racial Castration: Managing Masculinity in Asian America.* Durham, N.C.: Duke University Press, 2001.

Eriksen, Thomas Hylland. *Ethnicity and Nationalism: Anthropological Perspectives.* London: Pluto Press, 1993.

Fairmann, John. *Cheap Sugar or Coolie Immigration to the West Indies: In a Series of Letters.* Reprinted from "The Witness." Edinburgh: Paton and Ritchie, 1859.

Fanon, Frantz. "The Fact of Blackness." In *Black Skin, White Masks,* translated by Charles Lam Markmann, 109–140. London: Pluto Press, 1986.

———. "On National Culture." In *The Wretched of the Earth,* translated by Constance Farrington, preface by Jean-Paul Sartre, 206–248. New York: Grove Press, 1963.

———. "The Pitfalls of National Consciousness." In *The Wretched of the Earth,* 148–205.

Gellner, Ernest. *Nations and Nationalism.* Ithaca, N.Y.: Cornell University Press, 1983.

Geok-lin Lim, Shirley. "Feminist and Ethnic Literary Theories in Asian American Literature." *Feminist Studies* 19, no. 3 (1993): 571–595.

Gilroy, Paul. *The Black Atlantic: Modernity and Double Consciousness.* Cambridge: Harvard University Press, 1993.

Goh, Robbie B. H., and Shawn Wong, eds. *Asian Diasporas: Cultures, Identities, Representations.* Hong Kong: Hong Kong University Press, 2004.

Green, William A. "Emancipation to Indenture: A Question of Imperial Morality." *Journal of British Studies* 22, no. 2 (1983): 98–121.

———. "The West Indies and Indentured Labor Migration—The Jamaican Experience." *Indentured Labor in the British Empire,* edited by Kay Saunders, 1–41.

Guibernau, Montserrat. *Nationalisms: The Nation-State and Nationalism in the Twentieth Century.* Cambridge: Polity Press, 1996.

Hall, Laura J. "The Chinese in Guyana: The Making of a Creole Community." Ph.D. diss., University of California at Berkeley, Ethnic Studies Graduate Division, 1995.

Hall, Stuart. "Cultural Identity and Diaspora." In *Theorizing Diaspora,* edited by Jana Evans Braziel and Anita Mannur, 233–246. Malden, Mass.: Blackwell, 2003.

———. "New Ethnicities." In *Black British Cultural Studies: A Reader,* edited by Houston A. Baker Jr., Manthia Diawara, and Ruth H. Lindeborg, 163–172. Chicago: University of Chicago Press, 1996.

Hedrick, Tace. *Mestizo Modernism: Race, Nation, and Identity in Latin American Culture, 1900–1940*. New Brunswick, N.J.: Rutgers University Press, 2003.

Higman, B. W. "The Chinese in Trinidad, 1806–1838." *Caribbean Studies* 12, no. 3 (1972): 21–44.

Hintzen, Percy C. "Race and Creole Ethnicity in the Caribbean." In *Questioning Creole*, edited by Shepherd and Richards, 92–110.

Ho, Christine. "Creolization of the Chinese in Guyana, Trinidad, and Jamaica." In *Caribbean Asians: Chinese, Indian and Japanese Experiences in Trinidad and the Dominican Republic*, edited by Roger Sanjek. 31–61. New York: Queens College, CUNY, Asian/American Center at Queens College, 1990.

———. "'Hold the Chow Mein, Gimme Soca': Creolization of the Chinese in Guyana, Trinidad, and Jamaica." *Amerasia* 15, no. 2 (1989): 3–25.

Hobsbawm, Eric J. "Introduction: Inventing Traditions." In *The Invention of Tradition*, edited by Eric Hobsbawm and Terence Ranger, 1–14. Cambridge: Cambridge University Press, 1995.

———. *Nations and Nationalism since 1780: Programme, Myth, Reality*. Cambridge: Cambridge University Press, 1990.

Hopkins, Nick, and Christopher Moore. "Categorizing the Neighbors: Identity, Distance, and Stereotyping." *Social Psychology Quarterly* 64, no. 3 (2001): 239–252.

Hufford, Mary. "Context." *Journal of American Folklore* 108, no. 430 (1995): 528–549.

Hutchinson, John, and Anthony D. Smith. *Ethnicity*. Oxford: Oxford University Press, 1996.

Jagan, Cheddi. *Forbidden Freedom: The Story of British Guiana*. Reprint. London: Hansib; Coolie Odyssey, 1989.

Jameson, Fredric. "Third World Literature in the Era of Multinational Capitalism." *Social Text*, no. 15 (1986): 65–88.

Jenkins, Edward. *The Coolie: His Rights and Wrongs*. New York: George Routledge and Sons, 1871.

———. *The Coolie in Demerara: A Few Words Upon "The Coolie, His Rights and Wrongs" by the Author of "Ginx's Baby."* London: Spottiswoode, 1871.

———. *Lutchmee and Dilloo: A Study of West Indian Life in Three Volumes*. London: William Mullan & Son, 1877.

Jin, Meiling. "Short Fuse." In *Song of the Boatwoman*, 87–97. Leeds: Peepal Tree Press, 1996.

———. "Victoria." In *Song of the Boatwoman*, 7–22.

Johnson, Howard. "The Anti-Chinese Riots of 1918 in Jamaica." *Caribbean Quarterly* 28, no. 3 (1982): 19–32.

———. "The Chinese in Trinidad in the Late Nineteenth Century." *Ethnic and Racial Studies* 10, no. 1 (1987): 82–95.

Johnson, Joyce. "Representations of the Chinese in Anglophone Caribbean Fiction." *Immigrants and Minorities* 16, no. 3 (1997): 36–54.

Johnson, Kim. *Descendants of the Dragon: The Chinese in Trinidad, 1806–2006*. Kingston: Ian Randle, 2006.

Kapchan, Deborah A. "Performance." *Journal of American Folklore* 108, no. 430 (1995): 479–508.

Kedourie, Elie. *Nationalism*. Oxford: Blackwell, 1994.

Khan, Ismith. "The Magic Ring." In *A Day in the Country and Other Stories*, 34–52. Leeds: Peepal Tree Books, 1994.

Kim, Elaine H. "Defining Asian American Realities through Literature." *Cultural Critique*, no. 6 (1987): 87–111.

———. "'Such Opposite Creatures': Men and Women in Asian American Literature." *Michigan Quarterly* 29, no. 1 (1990): 68–93.

Kingsley, Charles. *At Last: A Christmas in the West Indies*. London: Macmillan, 1889.

Kirke, Henry. *Twenty-Five Years in British Guiana*. London: Sampson Low, Marston, 1898.

Kirkpatrick, Margery. *From the Middle Kingdom to the New World: Aspects of the Chinese Experience in Migration to British Guiana*. Vol. 1. Georgetown, Guyana: Margery Kirkpatrick, 1993.

Kondo, Dorinne. "(Re)Visions of Race: Contemporary Race Theory and the Cultural Politics of Racial Crossing in Documentary Theatre." *Theatre Journal* 52, no. 1 (2000): 81–107.

Kushigian, Julia A. *Orientalism in the Hispanic Literary Tradition: In Dialogue with Borges, Paz, and Sarduy*. Albuquerque: University of New Mexico Press, 1991.

———. "'Ríos en la noche: Fluyen los jardines': Orientalism in the work of Octavio Paz." *Hispania* 70, no. 4 (1987): 776–786.

Kwok Crawford, Marlene. *Scenes from the History of the Chinese in Guyana*. Georgetown, Guyana: Marlene Kwok Crawford, 1989.

Laurence, K. O. *Immigration into the West Indies in the 19th Century*. Kingston: Caribbean Universities Press, 1979.

———. *A Question of Labor: Indentured Immigration into Trinidad and British Guiana, 1875–1917*. Kingston: Ian Randle, 1994.

Lee, Easton. *From Behind the Counter: Poems from a Rural Jamaican Experience*. Kingston: Ian Randle, 1998.

———. *Heritage Call: Ballad for the Children of the Dragon*. Kingston: Ian Randle, 2001.

Lee, Erika. "Orientalisms in the Americas: A Hemispheric Approach to Asian American History." *Journal of Asian American Studies* 8, no. 3 (2005): 235–256.

Lee, Regina. "Theorizing Diasporas." In *Asian Diasporas, Cultures, Identities, Representations*, edited by Robbie B. H. Goh and Shawn Wong, 53–76. Hong Kong: Hong Kong University Press, 2004.

Lee, Robert G. *Oriental: Asian Americans in Popular Culture*. Philadelphia: Temple University Press, 1999.

Lee, Tom Yin. *The Chinese in Jamaica*. Kingston: Lee Tom Yin, 1957.

Lee-Loy, Anne-Marie. "'. . . The Chinese are Preferred to all Others': Nineteenth-Century Representations of the Chinese in Trinidad and British Guiana." *Asian Studies Review* 27, no. 2 (2003): 205–225.

———. "The Chinese Shop as Nation Theatre in West Indian Literature." *Anthurium: A Caribbean Studies Journal* 5, no. 1 (2007). 14 pars. http://anthurium.miami.edu/volume_5/issue_1/leeloy-chineseshop.html.

———. "An Interview with Janice Lowe Shinebourne." *Arts Journal* 4, no. 1/2 (2008): 39–44.

———. "Kissing the Cross: Nineteenth-Century Representations of Chinese and Indian Immigrants in Trinidad and British Guiana." In *The Chinese in the Caribbean*, edited by A. Wilson, 25–39. Princeton, N.J.: M. Wiener, 2004.

Lind, Andrew W. "Adjustment Patterns Among the Jamaican Chinese." *Social and Economic Studies* 7, no. 2 (1958): 144–164.

Look Lai, Walton. "The Caribbean." In *The Encyclopedia of the Chinese Overseas*, edited by Lynn Pan, 248–253. Surrey: Curzon Press, 1998.

———. "Chinese Indentured Labor Migrations to the British West Indies in the Nineteenth Century." In *Caribbean Asians: Chinese, Indian, and Japanese Experiences in Trinidad and the Dominican Republic*, ed. Sanjek, 3–30.

———. *The Chinese in the West Indies, 1806–1995. A Documentary History*. Barbados, Jamaica and Trinidad and Tobago: The Press University of the West Indies, 1998.

———. *Indentured Labor, Caribbean Sugar. Chinese and Indian Migrants to the British West Indies, 1838–1918*. Baltimore and London: The Johns Hopkins University Press, 1993.

———, ed. *Essays on the Chinese Diaspora in the Caribbean.* St. Augustine, Trinidad: History Department, University of the West Indies, 2006.

Lopez, Kathleen. "The Chinese in Cuban History." *Essays on the Chinese Diaspora in the Caribbean,* edited by Look Lai, 105–129.

López-Calvo, Ignacio. *Imaging the Chinese in Cuban Literature and Culture.* Gainesville: University Press of Florida, 2008.

Lowenthal, David. *West Indian Societies.* London: Oxford University Press, 1972.

Lynch-Campbell, H. *Chinese in Jamaica.* Kingston: City Printery, 1975.

Mahon, Maureen. "The Visible Evidence of Cultural Producers." *Annual Review of Anthropology* 29 (2000): 467–492.

Mais, Roger. *The Hills Were Joyful Together.* Caribbean Writers Series. Kingston: Heinemann, 1981.

Marshall, Paule. "British Guiana." In *Soul Clap Hands and Sing,* 67–127. Washington, D.C.: Howard University Press, 1988.

McKenzie, Alecia. *Satellite City and Other Stories.* Essex: Longman Group UK, 1992.

McKenzie, Earl. "Platform Shoes." In *Two Roads to Mount Joyful and Other Stories,* 46–57. Essex: Longman Group UK, 1992.

Meagher, Arnold J. *The Coolie Trade: The Traffic in Chinese Laborers to Latin America, 1847–1874.* Philadelphia: Xlibris Corporation, 2008.

Mendes, Alfred H. *Black Fauns.* London: New Beacon Books, 1984.

———. "Her Chinaman's Way." In *From Trinidad: An Anthology of Early West Indian Writing,* edited by Reinhard W. Sander, 103–118. Kent: Hodder and Stoughton, 1978.

———. *Pitch Lake.* London: New Beacon Books, 1980.

Millet, Trevor. "The Chinese Community in Trinidad and Tobago: A Case Study of a Commercial Ethnic Minority." In *Entrepreneurship in the Caribbean: Culture, Structure, Conjuncture,* edited by Selwyn Ryan and Taimoon Stewart, 177–202. St. Augustine, Trinidad: University of the West Indies, 1994.

Millett, Trevor M. *The Chinese in Trinidad.* Port of Spain: Imprint Caribbean, 1993.

Mintz, Sidney W. "Caribbean Nationhood: An Anthropological Perspective." In *Caribbean Transformations,* 302–328. Baltimore: Johns Hopkins University Press, 1984.

Mittelholzer, Edgar. *A Morning in the Office.* Caribbean Writers Series. London: Heinemann, 1974.

Mordecai, Martin. "Chinyman." *Caribbean Quarterly* 15, no. 4 (1969): 40.

Moore, Brian L. *Cultural Power, Resistance, and Pluralism: Colonial Guyana, 1838–1900.* Barbados, Jamaica, and Trinidad and Tobago: The Press University of the West Indies; and Montreal and Kingston, London and Buffalo: McGill-Queen's University Press, 1995.

———. *Race, Power, and Social Segmentation in Colonial Society. Guyana after Slavery, 1838–1891.* Philadelphia: Gordon and Breach, 1987.

Murdoch, H. Adlai. "Rhys's Pieces: Unhomeliness as Arbitrator of Caribbean Creolization." *Callaloo* 26, no. 1 (2003): 252–272.

Naipaul, Shiva. "The Beauty Contest." In *A Man of Mystery and Other Stories,* 1–11. London: Penguin, 1984.

Naipaul, V. S. "The Baker's Story." In *The Penguin Book of Caribbean Short Stories,* edited by E. A. Markham, 165–175. London: Penguin, 1996.

———. *Guerrillas.* London: André Deutsch, 1975.

———. *Miguel Street.* London: Penguin, 1959.

Nash, Manning. "The Core Elements of Ethnicity." In *Ethnicity,* edited by John Hutchinson and Anthony D. Smith 24–28. Oxford: Oxford University Press, 1996.

Nettleford, Rex. *Mirror, Mirror: Identity, Race, and Protest in Jamaica.* Kingston: William Collins and Sangster, 1970.

Nguyen, Viet Thanh. "The Remasculinization of Chinese America: Race, Violence, and the Novel." *American Literary History* 12, no. 1/2 (2000): 130–157.

Norman Washington Manley and the New Jamaica: Selected Speeches and Writings, 1938–1968. Edited by Rex Nettleford. New York: Africana, 1971.

Nunez, Elizabeth. *Bruised Hibiscus.* New York: Ballantine, 2000.

Oxaal, Ivar. *Black Intellectuals Come to Power: The Rise of Creole Nationalism in Trinidad and Tobago.* Cambridge: Schenkman, 1968.

Palumbo-Liu, David. "The Minority Self as Other: Problematics of Representation in Asian American Literature." *Cultural Critique,* no. 28 (1994): 75–102.

Parreñas, Rhacel S., and Lok C. D. Siu, eds. *Asian Diasporas: New Formations, New Conceptions.* Stanford: Stanford University Press, 2007.

Patrick Jones, Marion. *Pan Beat.* Port of Spain: Columbus, 1973.

Patterson, Orlando. "Context and Choice in Ethnic Allegiance: A Theoretical Framework and Caribbean Case Study." In *Ethnicity: Theory and Experience,* edited by Nathan Glazer and Daniel P. Moynihan, 303–349. Cambridge, Mass.: Harvard University Press, 1975.

Powell, Patricia. *The Pagoda.* San Diego: Harcourt Brace, 1998.

Poynting, Jeremy. "'You Want to Be a Coolie Woman?' Gender and Ethnic Identity in Indo-Caribbean Women's Writing." In *Caribbean Women Writers: Essays from the First International Conference,* edited by Selwyn Cudjoe, 98–105. Wellesley, Mass.: Calaloux, 1990.

Reckford, Michael. "Dog Food." In *The Faber Book of Contemporary Caribbean Short Stories,* edited by Mervyn Morris, 175–180. London: Faber and Faber, 1990.

Rohlehr, Gordon. "The Culture of Williams: Context, Performance, Legacy." *Callaloo* 20, no. 4 (1997): 849–888.

Rooplall, Monar. "Money Can't Play." In *Estate People,* 9–15. Georgetown, Guyana: Roraima, 1994.

Royal Gazette, 1850, 1853, 1870, 1874. Caribbean Views Collection. British Library (Newspaper). Colindale, London.

Said, Edward. *Orientalism.* New York: Vintage, 1979.

Salih, Sara, ed., with Judith Butler. *The Judith Butler Reader.* Malden, Mass.: Blackwell, 2004.

Selvon, Samuel. *A Brighter Sun.* Essex: Pearson, 1985.

———. "Highway in the Sun." In *Highway in the Sun. A Collection of Plays,* 4–52. Leeds: Peepal Tree Press, 1991.

———. "Song of Sixpence." In *The Penguin Book of Caribbean Short Stories,* 134–145.

———. *Turn Again Tiger.* Port of Spain and Kingston: Heinemann, n.d.

Senior, Olive. "The Tenantry of Birds." In *Arrival of the Snake Woman and Other Stories,* 46–61. Essex: Longman Group UK, 1989.

Sewell, W. *The Ordeal of Free Labor in the British West Indies.* New York: Harper and Brothers, 1861.

Shaw, Thomas A. "To Be or Not to Be Chinese: Differential Expressions of Chinese Culture and Solidarity in the British West Indies." In *Caribbean Ethnicity Revisited,* edited by Stephen Glazier, 71–185. New York: Gordon and Breach, 1985.

Shinebourne, Janice. "The Berbice Marriage Match" In *The Godmother and Other Stories,* 103–112. Leeds: Peepal Tree Press, 2004.

———. *The Last English Plantation.* Leeds: Peepal Tree Press, 1988.

———. "London and New York." In *The Godmother and Other Stories,* 95–101.

———. *Timepiece.* Leeds: Peepal Tree Press, n.d.

Siu, Lok C. D. *Memories of a Future Home: Diasporic Citizenship of Chinese in Panama*. Stanford: Stanford University Press, 2005.

Smith, Anthony D. "Introduction: Ethnicity and Nationalism." In *Ethnicity and Nationalism*, edited by Anthony D. Smith, 1–4. Leiden: E. J. Brill, 1992.

———. *The Ethnic Origin of Nations*. Oxford: Blackwell, 1986.

———. "The Nation: Invented, Imagined, Reconstructed?" In *Re-Imagining the Nation*, edited by Marjorie Kingrose and Adam J. Lerner, 9–28. Buckingham: Open University Press, 1993.

———. *National Identity*. London: Penguin, 1991.

Smith, M. G. *The Plural Society in the British West Indies*. Berkeley: University of California Press, 1965.

Standish, Robert. *Mr. On Loong*. London: Peter Davies, 1950.

Stanley, E. *Claims and Resources of the West Indian Colonies: A Letter*. London: T. & W. Boone, 1850.

"Stewart Brown Interviews Willi Chen, Author of *The King of the Carnival* (Hansib 1988)." *Journal of West Indian Literature* 5, no. 1/ 2 (1992): 106–112.

Striff, Erin, ed. *Performance Studies*. New York: Palgrave Macmillan, 2003.

Strongman, Roberto. "A Caribbean Response to the Question of Third World National Allegories: Jameson, Ahmad, and the Return of the Repressed." *Anthurium: A Caribbean Studies Journal* 6, no. 2 (2008). 44 pars. http://anthurium.miami.edu/volume_6/issue_2/strongman-acarribeanresponse.html.

Sue-A-Quan, Trev. *Cane Reapers: Chinese Indentured Immigrants in Guyana*. Vancouver: Riftswood, 1999.

Szeman, Imre. *Zones of Instability: Literature, Postcolonialism, and the Nation*. Baltimore: Johns Hopkins University Press, 2003.

Tarica, Estelle. *The Inner Life of Mestizo Nationalism*. Minneapolis: University of Minnesota Press, 2008.

Tindall, William York. "The Sociological Best Seller." *College English* 9, no. 2 (1947): 55–62.

Tiryakian, Edward A. "The Wild Cards of Modernity." *Daedalus* 126, no. 2 (1997): 145–181.

Trollope, Anthony. *The West Indies and the Spanish Main*. Reprint. London: Frank Cass, 1968.

Underhill, Edward Bean. *The West Indies: Their Social and Religious Condition*. Westport, Conn.: Negro Universities Press, 1970.

Wallerstein, Immanuel. "The Construction of Peoplehood: Racism,

Nationalism, Ethnicity." In *Race, Nation, Class. Ambiguous Identities*, 71–85.

Walrond, Eric. "The Wharf Rats." In *The Penguin Book of Caribbean Short Stories*, 95–106.

Webber, A. R. F. *Centenary History and Handbook of British Guiana.* British Guiana: Argosy, 1931.

Westall, Claire. "Men in the Yard and on the Street: Cricket and Calypso in Moon on a Rainbow Shawl and Miguel Street." *Anthurium: A Caribbean Studies Journal* 3, no. 2 (2005). 13 pars. http://anthurium.miami.edu/volume_3/issue_2/westall-meninthe.htm.

Williams, Eric. *History of the People of Trinidad and Tobago.* Port of Spain: PNM, 1962.

———. *Inward Hunger: The Education of a Prime Minister.* 2nd ed. Chicago: University of Chicago Press, 1971.

Williams, N. D. *Ikael Torass.* Havana: Casa de las Américas, 1976.

Wilson, A., ed. *The Chinese in the Caribbean.* Princeton, N.J.: M. Wiener, 2004:

Wirth-Nesher, Hana. "The Cause of Marginality: Colonialism in Naipaul's *Guerrillas*." *MFS (Modern Fiction Studies)* 30, no. 3 (1984): 531–545.

Woodroffe, Noel. "Wing's Way." In *Best West Indian Stories*, 138–144.

Wong, Sau-ling, and Jeffrey J. Santa Ana. "Gender and Sexuality." *Signs* 25, no. 1 (1999): 171–226.

Wurgaf, Lewis D. "Identity in World History: A Postmodern Perspective." *History and Theory* 34, no. 2 (1995): 67–85.

Wynter, Sylvia. *The Hills of Hebron.* Longman Drumbeat. Essex: Longman Group, 1984.

Yu, Ouyang. "All the Lower Orders: Representations of the Chinese Cook, Market Gardeners, and Other Lower-Class People in Australian Literature from 1888 to 1988." *Kunapipi* 15, no. 3 (1993): 21–34.

Yun, Lisa. "An Afro-Chinese Caribbean: Cultural Cartographies of Contrariness in the Work of Antonio Chuffat Latour, Margaret Cezair-Thompson, and Patricia Powell. *Caribbean Quarterly* 50, no. 2 (2004): 26–34.

———. "Chinese Coolies and African Slaves in Cuba, 1847–1874." *Journal of Asian American Studies* 4, no. 2 (2001): 99–122.

———. *The Coolie Speaks: Chinese Indentured Laborers and African Slaves in Cuba.* Philadelphia: Temple University Press, 2008.

———. "Under the Hatches: American Coolie Ships and Nineteenth

Century Narratives of the Passage." *Amerasia Journal* 28, no. 2 (2002): 38–63.

Zahlan, Anne R. "Literary Murder: V. S. Naipaul's *Guerrillas.*" *South Atlantic Review* 59, no. 4 (1994): 89–106.

Interviews, Conversations, and E-mail

Conversation with Easton Lee, Kingston, Jamaica, 12 July 2002.

Conversation with Willi Chen, Coventry, UK, 30 July 2002 (by phone).

Conversation with Victor Chang, Kingston, Jamaica, 12 July 2002.

E-mail from Willi Chen, 3 August 2002.

Manuscript Collections

Parliamentary Papers (PP), vol. 35, Correspondence Relative to Emigration of Laborers to the West Indies and the Mauritius from the West Coast of Africa, the East Indies, and China, 1844 (Chadwyck-Healey 48.291–48.292).

Parliamentary Papers, vol. 68, Copies or Extracts of Despatches Relating to Chinese Immigrants Recently Introduced into the Colonies of British Guiana and Trinidad, August 1853 (Chadwyck-Healey 57.500–57.502).

Parliamentary Papers, vol. 27, Fourteenth General Report of the Colonial Land and Emigration Commissioners, 1854 (Chadwyck-Healey 58.239–78.241).

Parliamentary Papers, vol. 20, Report of the Commissioners to Enquire into the Treatment of Immigrants in British Guiana, June 1871 (Chadwyck-Healey, 77.174–77.178).

Public Record Office (PRO), Colonial Office, CO 295/14, CO 295/15, CO 295/16, CO 295/17, CO 295/18, CO 295/222.

Index

About the Author

Anne-Marie Lee-Loy is an Assistant Professor in the Department of English at Ryerson University.